# ...LKIRK TALKS

A social history of
the Oxton area

By **Henry Borthwick**

Illustrated by **Elspeth Borthwick**
and **Kevin Osborn**

Production: Michael Gill/Fiona Laing/Dick Pringle
Cover: michaelgill.eu
Print: Kelso Graphics LLP
The Knowes, Kelso, Scottish Borders TD5 7BH
e: admin@kelsographics.co.uk   t: 01573 223214

*First Edition*
*June 2010*

ISBN No. is 978-0-9565899-0-3

# Contents

*Foreward*                                                                4

*Author's note*                                                           5

*Acknowledgements*                                                        6


Chapter 1: *Layers of history: Romans, religion and roads*               9

Chapter 2: *History of the Church*                                       39

Chapter 3: *Some ministers and their times*                              51

Chapter 4: *Channelkirk graves*                                          63

Chapter 5: *Upper Lauderdale and the Soutra Plateau*                     73

Chapter 6: *The area around Oxton and the Railway*                       95

Chapter 7: *The Village of Oxton*                                       109


*Epilogue*                                                              130


*Appendix 1 – Lammermoor Leaves*                                        131

*Appendix 2 – Tourist Information for the Lauder Light  Railway*         143

*Appendix 3 – Colonel Guinan's Letter*                                  145


*Bibliography*                                                          148

*List of illustrations*                                                 150


*Index*                                                                 155

# An Appreciation

EVERY Border village has one or more local historians who collect the tools and tales of bygone times from their own area. Some write these down in notebooks which often get thrown away; some take their collected knowledge to the grave and only fragments are remembered for a short time. A few take the time to write them down and get them published in book form so that their knowledge and experiences can be passed on to future generations.

Henry Borthwick has taken the trouble to turn his series of talks about Channelkirk into an interesting book called, appropriately, *Channelkirk Talks.* His family have been associated with the area since 1458 and, as a descendant of Robert Borthwick, the Master Gunner at the Battle of Flodden who could have won a victory at that battle if only James IV had listened to his urgent plea to be allowed to fire on the English army while they were still assembling, Henry Borthwick is well-placed to comment on the history of the parish.

But this is not merely a historical commentary. It records the social life of Channelkirk and Oxton, telling of the triumphs and disasters, even boredoms of the everyday life of the ordinary people who inhabited the village of Oxton, which is still there, and that of Channelkirk, which has long since vanished. It notes the changing scene in the countryside over the last century and brings to the mind some of the characters who lived in it.

It is a good book, full of facts and reminiscences and will be valuable source material for future social historians. I hope someone will write the next chapter, say, in 2077.

*Walter Elliot*

# Author's note

THE information in this book is based on a series of talks about Channelkirk which I gave at local venues between 2001 and 2006, hence the title of the book. It is not intended to be a definitive social history of Channelkirk Parish or the Oxton area. I only touch on a few facts and stories.

Channelkirk history is well documented in books such as *History of Channelkirk, Channelkirk Clippings* and *Lauderdale in the 20th Century,* but many of the stories in this book have remained dormant or unprinted until now.

In recent years, there has been an upsurge of interest in local history and this has been borne out by fact that the Lauderdale Historical Society was inaugurated in 2003.

This book has mainly been compiled using readily available sources of information. Since moving to the Oxton area in 1977, I found that there was a wealth of knowledge held by some long-time residents. I have tried to avoid using too many names of people and places and giving too many dates. While most of the book refers to people and events within the parish of Channelkirk, there are some events which take place on the fringes of the parish and further afield. I have added a little of my family history where appropriate. We have been associated with Channelkirk since 1458.

There are three owners of copyrights which I have been unable to trace. These are: a) Photograph of tossing the caber at the Oxton Games, August 1936; b) Text from *The Scottish Castle* by Stewart Cruden published in 1960 by Nelson, and, c) Text from Wilson's *Tales of the Borders* by John Mackay Wilson published in 1934 by The Murray Press. If anyone can help, I would be grateful.

Any profits from the sale of *Channelkirk Talks* will be donated to charity.

# Acknowledgements

THIS book could not have been written without the help and support of many people and organisations. I wish to acknowledge some of my main sources of information from published material, which are:

The Rev. Archibald Allan – *History of Channelkirk*, particularly for information concerning Channelkirk Church; John Mackay – Illustrated articles describing local people, places and events, mainly published in the *Scots Magazine*; John James Mackay – Description of the road over Soutra and information on transport from his book *Border Highways*; Scotsman Publications and the *Southern Reporter* – Local newspaper articles; Lilian Groves – Information on the life of St Cuthbert; Brian Moffat – Information on the Soutra Hospital/Hospice and other information on Soutra; Ian Landells – Poetry printed in Appendix 1; Catherine Reid – Great granddaughter of Will H Ogilvie for permission to quote a verse of his poetry.

Information from other publications are acknowledged where appropriate, and further information about books are included in the Bibliography.

I would also like to convey my grateful thanks to many individuals and hope the following list omits none: Walter Elliot, Donald Gordon, Ernie Miller, Elizabeth Redpath, Nicola Ireland, David Muir, Malcolm Borthwick, John Gilchrist, Brian Moffat, Dave Waldie, Harry Borthwick, Jean Blades, Ian Sutherland, Sandy Sutherland, Tom Cuthell, Josh Bennet, Drew Kellet, William Bortrick, Lindsay Errington, Richard Robbins, Ann Longden, Ian Landells, Jean Scott, Harry Crombie Smith, Mary Sutherland, James Spence, Margery Bennet, John Hunt, Johnnie Weir, John Mitchell, Flora Pretswell, Lesley Caithness, John Wilkinson, Alice Wilkinson, Morag Cunningham, Ron Hill, Dod Gilchrist, David Murray, Andy Gilchrist, Sheila Laing, Alice Telford, Liz Leeming,

David Thomson, Alec Sked, Kevin Osborn, Dick Pringle, Liz Taylor, Kenny Walker, Jack Tully-Jackson, Andy Hume, Tony Guinan, Alastair Cormack, Alec McDonald, John Moffat, Edna Hill and Caroline Buchanan.

In addition, I am greatly indebted to Walter Elliot for his agreement to write the foreword. He is a well known historian and has published a number of books as well as delivering a series of broadcasts on the radio.

Finally, on a more personal note, I should like to acknowledge the encouragement and tolerance shown by my wife Elspeth who, apart from suffering all the inconveniences of the more anti-social aspects of preparation for the series of talks and writing this book, has agreed to add some sketches. I dedicate this book to her.

*Henry Borthwick*

# Layers of history: Romans, religion and roads

## A circular parish

From the heights of the Lammermuirs to the flatter lands of Lauderdale, Channelkirk Parish is a circular area approximately 10 km (6 miles) in diameter. It lies to the south-east of Edinburgh, with the centre of population Oxton Village 34 km (21 miles) from the Scottish capital (Plates 1 and 2, over page). It is bounded by the parishes of Lauder, Stow, Fala and Humbie.

The parish is situated in the Lammermuir Hills and has long depended on agriculture, mainly sheep. Most of the ground is hilly with heather and Blackface sheep on the higher summits. Most hill farms also carry a small herd of cattle.

In the north of the parish lies the Soutra Plateau which is generally over 360 metres (1,180 ft) above sea level. In the south lies the flatter land of Lauderdale, situated either side of the river

Plate 1: Oxton painted by John Mackay. Reproduced courtesy of Liz Maddock

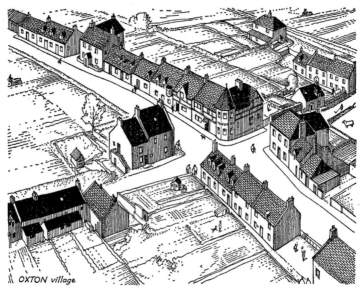

Plate 2: Drawing of Oxton Village by John Mackay, 1974

Leader at a height of 190 metres (620 ft) as it leaves the parish. This lower land is of a more arable nature. Crops of barley, turnips, hay and silage are grown in the parish for feeding cattle and sheep in the winter. Some of the names in the area reflect the importance of sheep, such as Lammermuir, Hog Hill and Collie Law.

Travelling north on the A68 from Lauder to Pathhead, the road enters Channelkirk parish beside the Leader Water just south of the junction with the A697 road (Map 1). The A68 proceeds in a north-westerly direction passing Oxton road-end and climbing Upper Lauderdale with Glengelt then Turf Law summit on the west side and New Channelkirk and Headshaw then Headshaw Hill on the east side and winds up on to the Soutra Plateau leaving the

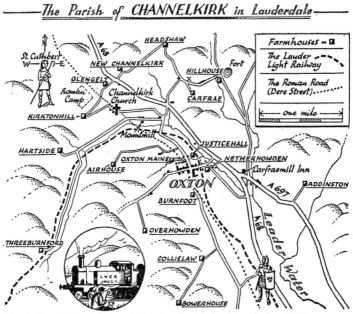

Map 1: The Parish of Channelkirk in Lauderdale by John Mackay, 1974

Plate 3 (left): Looking down Upper Lauderdale with Scots Pine trees in foreground

Plate 4 (below): Part of the Fort on Dere Street lying NNW from Kirktonhill. In the foreground is a farm vehicle track

parish just north of the derelict buildings of Hunters Hall.

Upper Lauderdale (Plate 3) and the Soutra Plateau, while not being official names, describe the steep-sided upper part of the Lauderdale valley and the high flattish boggy land on either side of the road respectively. After leaving the parish the road winds down Soutra hill on its way to Pathhead and hence towards Edinburgh.

## Highway of history

Lauderdale is a highway of history. There is a lot of evidence of the Roman occupation within the parish. The first Roman incursion was probably 78AD or 79AD when Julius Agricola, passing through Roxburghshire on his way to Edinburgh, proceeded north by Channelkirk. In Roman times, road makers crossed Soutra as part of Dere Street. Dere Street went from the Tees to the Forth. The line of the Roman road probably went through the dining room of the former manse next door to the church. Recently, Historic Scotland put up a sign about 1.2 km (0.75 mile) to the north-west of the church, which lies south-west of the summit of Turf Law. The sign indicates the route and profile of the Roman road. In places, the construction of the road can be made out.

On Dere Street, about 400 metres north-west of this Historic Scotland sign, is a fort. It is difficult to establish whether this is a Roman or a native hill fort of the 2nd Century without excavating the site. The double ditches round the perimeter are in a well preserved state and the fort is positioned on a strategic site (Plate 4). It is not mentioned in any map that I have seen, but would fit in with the pattern and position of similar Roman forts. Unfortunately, trees have been planted over half of the site. On the opposite side of Dere Street, but nearer the Historic Scotland sign, are a series of

13

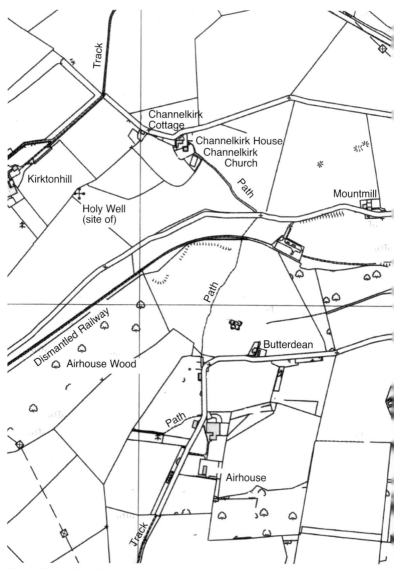

Map 2: Channelkirk Church and surrounding area. © Crown Copyright and/or database right. All rights reserved. Licence No. 100046429

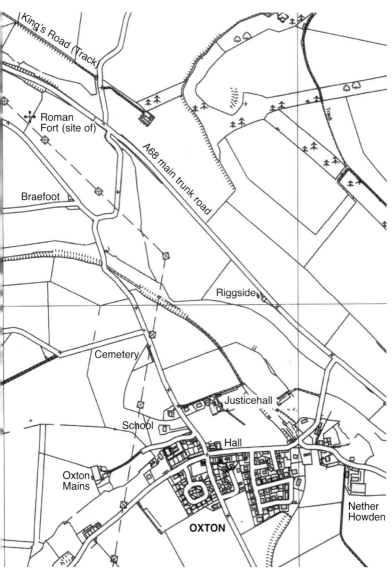

Map 3: Oxton and surrounding area. © Crown Copyright and/or database right.
All rights reserved. Licence No. 100046429

burial mounds, perhaps connected with the building of Dere Street.

In the immediate vicinity of Channelkirk Church, there had been a Roman fort with a series of walls and ditches. There was a temporary camp at Channelkirk lying immediately to the north-west of the church and extending to above Kirktonhill (Map 1, page 11). The camp would probably have housed upward of two Roman legions. This would have been 10,500 men. Details of some of the camp defences were seen from the air in the late 1940s.

The camp covered an area of approximately 67 hectares (165 acres). This is where Julius Agricola and his men could have spent some time on their way north. It is also possible that the camp dates from a later period.

## Roman camps

The line of Roman camps also includes temporary camps at St Leonards, Fala and Pathhead. There was generally a day's march between camps and at night they would have offered a safe resting place.

There is also a fort lying about 0.8 km (0.5 mile) east of the church. The double ditches round the fort are clearly discernable in aerial photographs (Plate 5, and Map 3, page 15). The fort is just above where Annfield Inn used to be.

No doubt the tribes round Channelkirk took part in many skirmishes with the Romans. The Romans tried again and again for 300 years to subdue the South of Scotland, but without any permanent success, In 116 AD the Ninth Legion set out from its base in York. It would appear to have reached the Roman fort at Trimontium at the base of the Eildon Hills near Newstead. The story goes that the entire legion disappeared without trace.

The late Mrs Brown dug up a coin of the Emperor Tiberius in her garden at Butterdean. The coin was bronze like an old penny. Butterdean (Map 2, page 14) is across the valley from the church and is thought to have been the place where women from the old village of Channelkirk used to wash their butter.

There have been a number of interesting Roman artefacts found in the south of Scotland. At the Roman fort of Trimontium, near Melrose, a ceremonial Roman helmet was excavated.

Plate 5: Aerial Photo of Oxton Fort. Annfield Inn in background. Taken in August 1956. University of Cambridge Photo Library Collection

17

The Border poet, Will H Ogilvie, wrote about the event in his poem *On a Roman Helmet* which starts:

> A helmet of the legion, this,
> That long and deep hath lain,
> Come back to taste the living kiss
> Of sun and wind again.
> Ah! touch it with a reverent hand,
> For in its burnished dome
> Lies here within this distant land
> The glory that was Rome!

There is a Roman Heritage Centre in Melrose which has information and exhibits on forts, settlements and artefacts connected with the area, including the Roman helmet.

(The two following paragraphs were taken from *Celtic Scotland*, written by Ian Armit, and can be found in Ch 4, p43 and Ch 1, p10 of his book): Roman writers had every reason to pronounce the Celts warlike, reckless and incapable of self-government. By doing so they could portray successive Roman advances as a positive contribution to the spread of civilized values.

Archaeology has often seemed to bear out their words. After all, the classic monument of the Iron Age is surely the hill fort, stoutly defended by rampart and ditch. But more recent studies have shown that the defensive capabilities of such sites were of secondary importance. The evolution of forts and enclosures does not, therefore, simply reflect the vagaries of warfare, but rather relates to the development of society itself. The Scots, Picts and Britons were all essentially Celtic, with their roots in the Europe-wide cultural traditions of the Iron Age.

For museum classification, the Iron Age is considered to be from

700BC until 500AD, which includes the Roman invasions of Britain.

Important Iron Age hill forts, settlements or meeting places are marked on Ordnance Survey maps. Within the borders of the Parish of Channelkirk there are sites of hill forts marked at Kirktonhill (Plate 6) and Hillhouse. There is also a hill fort marked at Tollishill, which is just outwith the parish boundary.

Aerial photography has revealed the existence of a levelled circular henge (circular earthwork) at Overhowden. This is a form of ceremonial monument which consists of a circular ditched enclosure with the upcast bank on the outer side. Such monuments were important meeting places for early farmers.

## The Kingdom of Bernicia

After the Romans had left Britain, the boundaries of the Kingdom of Bernicia came into existence in AD 547. This extended from the Tees to the Forth, thus embracing Channelkirk and, as a consequence, the area round Channelkirk was put under the

Plate 6: Part of the earthworks of the Celtic hillfort at Kirktonhill

domination of the Angles (English). In 559, this Kingdom seems to have been subsumed as a province within the greater Kingdom of Northumbria, stretching from the Forth to the Humber.

The information in the two paragraphs below comes from *The Triumph Tree* by Thomas Owen Clancy, first published in Great Britain by Canongate Books Ltd , 14 High Street, Edinburgh, EH1 1TE:

The most important work depicting the warfare between English and British kingdoms in the 6th Century is Aneirin's long poem, *The Gododdin.* It describes the utter defeat of a raiding party of British warriors drawn mainly from the kingdom of the Gododdin, based in Edinburgh.

The defeat happened at Catterick, in Yorkshire, but we do not know when, or much of the circumstances, outside of the poem's description of it. Still, it is a vivid realization of the violence of the time. It also indicates the direction in which the struggle was going against the ever-expanding English kingdoms, soon to be joined together as Northumbria. This defeat hastened the passing of an age for the British in the eastern lowlands of Scotland.

The language spoken by the local tribes would have been a Celtic one, an early form of Welsh. Some of the local names suggest that this is correct, for example, Trabroun was derived from Trefbrun, Threeburnford from Trefbrunforde (tref meaning settlement, brun meaning hill and forde meaning road).

There is a verse by Walter Elliot in his poem *Pure Border Scots* which sums up the situation.

> When the Romans left here, the tongue that was spoken
> Was a form o Welsh – an No! Ah'm no joken.
> Welsh lested a while until the time when

Some Germans sailed owre frae a place, Angeln.

Of course, they spoke German tho historians hide

An caa it "Old English" for the sake o' their pride.

The poem is contained in a recently published book called *The New Minstrelsy of the Scottish Border*, collected, compiled and written by Walter Elliot.

## Glen of terror

In the 7th Century, the valley landscape would have contained many more trees and marshy areas. At the top of Lauderdale is Glengelt, which translated is Glen Geilt – the glen of terror. Vagabonds and thieves would have inhabited the woods.

St Cuthbert, in the early part of his life, had connections with Channelkirk. Cuthbert was engaged under a master shepherd on the Channelkirk slopes. He was with other shepherds when he saw a vision in which the soul of Bishop Aidan of Lindisfarne was carried up to heaven. This would have been about 651 when Cuthbert was about 25 years old.

The shepherding in those days wasn't a peaceful, pastoral occupation, but one of protecting the flock from marauders and wild animals. There would have been wolves and wild boar. There might even have been brown bears. The last brown bear was killed in the 11th Century. Wild boar survived until the 16th Century, and wolves were on the brink of extinction by the end of the 17th Century.

## Monks and monasteries

It is clear from Bede's account that Cuthbert's life to that time had been preparing him for life as a monk, but it was this vision which confirmed God's calling to him to enter a monastery. Attracted by the reputation of Boisil, Prior of Melrose, Cuthbert rode off to that monastery and asked to be a novice. He is on horseback with a spear in his hand. Murder, revenge and plunder were rife in the district of the River Leader.

St Aidan founded the monastery at Melrose and its first Prior was Boisil. In those days, the monastery would have been a wooden construction about 2.4 km (1.5 miles) east of the present abbey. The name Mailros comes from the Welsh meaning "the bare promontory" and would have referred to Old Melrose where the monastery was situated below Scott's View.

After Cuthbert was professed as a monk he went with the monk Eata to the new monastery at Ripon. In 660, Eata fell out of favour with the king and together with Cuthbert and their fellow monks returned to Melrose.

Soon after his return, Cuthbert was struck down with the plague, which was sweeping the monastery. Many of his fellow monks died, but Cuthbert miraculously recovered. The Abbot Boisil, who himself caught the plague, told Cuthbert that he had been saved for a purpose. Boisil died, Eata became Abbot and Cuthbert became Prior of Melrose. St Cuthbert eventually became Abbot of Melrose. St Boisil gave his name to the town of St Boswells.

In 664, the King called a great Synod at Whitby. Here it was agreed that, henceforth, the Church of Northumbria should follow the continental practice. Colman, the Bishop of Lindisfarne, who was Irish, felt unable to accept the decision of the Synod of Whitby and he with other Irish monks and some English returned to Iona. Eata and Cuthbert were sent to Lindisfarne, and it fell to Cuthbert to persuade the remaining monks to accept the new practice. Many of the monks were unwilling to change their ways and Cuthbert declared that sometimes the seals listened more carefully than did the monks. However, Cuthbert never lost his temper and in the end brought them round. St Cuthbert went on to become Bishop of Lindisfarne and later retired to the Farne Islands.

The Inner Farne Island has a special association with St Cuthbert, who lived there from 676 to 684 and who after two years as Bishop of Lindisfarne returned to die there on 20 March, 687.

In 875, under threat of further attack from the Danes, the monks left Lindisfarne, taking with them the body of St Cuthbert, whose remains are now in Durham Cathedral. This is a story from a book called *The Abbeys of Melrose and Old Melrose* by John Bower printed in 1813.

The Venerable Bede relates a story in proof of St Cuthbert's holy life:

> He lived on the borders of the Picts, where a great multitude of people attended him in his devotions, and none ever returned from his instructions, but with great comfort and consolation. This caused him to be resorted to by old and young, they taking great pleasure both in hearing and seeing him. During this time it chanced that the daughter of the King of that part of the country became pregnant by some young man in her father's house.
>
> On the King perceiving it, and interrogating her strictly on the subject, she gave the following answer: "That solitary young man who dwelleth hard by is he who overcame me, and by whose beauty I was led astray." This still more incensed the King, who went immediately with his deflowered daughter, attended by sundry knights, to the place where the servant of

God was, whom he accosted in this manner, What! Art thou he, who, under the colour of religion, profanest the sanctuary of God? Art thou he, who, under the profession of a solitary life, exerciseth all the filthiness of the world? Behold my daughter, whom by thy deceit thou has corrupted; confess, therefore, before these witnesses, thy fault, and in what manner thou seducedst her."

The princess then, taking advantage of the blind rage of her father, impudently stepped forth and confirmed her assertion. On this the young man, greatly amazed, and knowing the accusation utterly false, looked up to God and prayed: "My Lord, my God, who knowest and art the searcher of all secrets, lay open this work of iniquity, and by some example prove this accusation false."

As soon as he had with tears and lamentations uttered these words, wonderful to behold, the earth on which the princess stood, making a hissing noise, suddenly opened and swallowed her up, in the view of all present. The King, struck with terror at what had happened, and in the utmost distress on account of his daughter, immediately, with all his company, implored pardon of God, and besought the holy St Cuthbert to intercede by his prayers with God for the restoration of the princess; which petition the holy father granted.

## The Dun Cow

The story of the Dun Cow goes that in 995, as the community of St Cuthbert was returning north after a few months in Ripon, the cart on which Cuthbert's coffin was carried stuck fast. After fasting and praying, one monk told Bishop Aldun that he had had a vision that

Cuthbert wanted to be buried on Dunholm. The puzzled monks heard two milkmaids talking about a cow which had wandered onto Dunholm. The excited community followed the milkmaids to the peninsula which became the final resting place of Cuthbert.

Without the life and death of a man who lived 1,300 years ago, there would have been no Durham Cathedral. Cuthbert's body was placed behind the high alter in the new Norman Cathedral in 1104 and there he still lies.

The following is from Sir Walter Scott's poem, *Marmion,* mentioning St Cuthbert:

> And, after many wanderings past,
> He chose his lordly seat at last,
> Where his cathedral, huge and vast,
> Looks down upon the Wear:
> There, deep in Durham's Gothic shade,
> His relics are in secret laid.

Looking up St Cuthbert on the internet, there is a story which relates that, while on a visit to the river Tyne, his prayers caused the wind to change so that a party of monks being swept out to sea on rafts were returned to safety. The monks were probably engaged in salmon fishing.

In the April 2002 edition of the Church of Scotland's magazine, *Life and Work,* a contributor's letter informed us that Cuthbert blessed the otters which were playing near him.

On a visit to the Royal Scottish Academy treasures stored in the basement of the Dean Gallery in Edinburgh, a small carved wooden sculpture came to my wife's attention. On further investigation, Elspeth noticed that it was a sculpture of St Cuthbert and that there were otters peeping out from below his robes. The carving was by

Plate 7: St Cuthbert and the otters. Photograph of Woodcarving by Elizabeth Strachan Dempster, circa 1950. Royal Scottish Academy Collection

Elizabeth Strachan Dempster (Plate 7).

From a Catholic Church document, the following story is told about St Cuthbert's stay at Lindisfarne:

And every night when his brethren were abed he would go and stand in cold water all naked up to his chin till it were midnight, and then he would issue out, and when he came to land he might not stand for feebleness and faintness, but oft fell down to the ground. And on a time as he lay thus, there came two otters which licked every place of his body, and then went again to the water that they came from. And then St Cuthbert arose all whole and went to his cell again, and went to matins with his brethren.

A bronze sculpture in Durham Cathedral shows Cuthbert as a much younger man, standing with the otters around his legs. He is also dressed as a bishop – early medieval style. The small sculpture is situated above the roll of honour of the Durham Light Infantry.

Many places have been named in memory of the saint, particularly holy places associated with his travels. One such place is Kirkcudbright. Cuthbert's nickname was "Cuddy".

We know from another chronicler, Coaevus Monachies, that during his stay in Mailros, Cuthbert was wont chiefly to resort to those places, and preach in such villages, as being seated high up and craggy, uncouth mountains, were frightful to others to behold and whose poverty and barbarity rendered them inaccessible to other teachers. Is this Channelkirk? Somebody commented to me recently that St Cuthbert was "a local boy made good".

I am indebted to Lilian Groves, Honorary Secretary of the Friends of Durham Cathedral, for information on St Cuthbert.

In 2006, the following article appeared in the Educational Section of *The Scotsman* newspaper. The first wonder in particular caught my attention:

*Wednesday, 5 April 2006*

**Small Wonders**

Young Scots took up our challenge to choose their Seven Wonders of Scotland, and there are some surprises here.

The Border Abbeys (Melrose Abbey)

The following story was written by an 11-year-old-boy from Kirk O' Shotts Primary School.

"I think Melrose Abbey is one of the Seven Wonders of Scotland because Melrose Abbey is beautiful and has lots and lots of history to it. Round about 1600 AD, there was a monk working in Melrose Abbey and he had very fat lips, so that goes to his nickname 'Fatlips'.

One day Fatlips was walking down into a chamber underneath the Abbey when Fatlips fell on the ground to his grave death. A few days later, an old lady said she wasn't scared of Fatlips and she entered the chamber too. A minute or two later, she came out screaming, shouting 'I've seen my death!' So to this day, hundreds of tourists come to Melrose Abbey for the beautiful view and for the haunting legend of Fatlips."

Next is a quotation from a school project-winning entry on

Melrose Abbey by a pupil, age nine, at St Mary's School, Melrose. "There are remains of gargoyles all around the Abbey. Gargoyles were made to keep away the evil spirits. One of the two remaining undamaged gargoyles is a pig playing the bagpipes." (A photograph of this gargoyle was included in the project).

About 300 metres to the west of Channelkirk Church there is a spring which bubbles up in a cleugh. This is marked on old maps as the Holy Water Cleugh. This is maybe where St Cuthbert had his vision and is also where early Christians were thought to have been baptized.

John Gilchrist, who was the Session Clerk of Channelkirk and the oldest person born in Oxton, has had all his family baptized with water from the Holy Water Cleugh.

In June 2005 the Oxton Community Council put up a plaque at the bottom of the Holy Water Cleugh which reads:

THE HALY WATTER CLEUCH
THE SPRING AT THE SOURCE OF
THIS BURN IS BELIEVED TO HAVE
BEEN WHERE SAINT CUTHBERT
BAPTISED HIS EARLY CONVERTS
TO THE CHRISTIAN FAITH
IN THE SEVENTH CENTURY A.D.

Recently there has been a way opened up from Melrose to Lindisfarne, called St Cuthbert's Way. This way is popular with walkers. Perhaps one day this will be from Channelkirk to Lindisfarne.

At the beginning of Appendix 1, there is a poem entitled *Old Airhouse Wood*, which follows in the footsteps of St Cuthbert. There is a short explanation of where Airhouse is located at the start of the Appendix. The Girthgate, or way by which the monks travelled from Melrose to Edinburgh, passes through the western border of the parish. Armstrong's map of the County of Berwick, dated 1771, shows the route of the Girthgate. It joins Dere Street as it climbs up to the watershed at Soutra. It may not have been much more than a footpath.

The name is thought to be derived from "garth", a place of sanctuary, and "gait", a way. On this road, a few kilometres due west of the church, are the ruins of an old building commonly called Restlaw Ha', at which, tradition says, the monks and pilgrims used to stop for refreshment. The few remains of Restlaw Ha' stand on Clints Hill close to the border with Hartside (Plate 8).

The monks maintained the Girthgate and some of them would have been journeying between the Cistercian abbeys of Newbattle and Melrose. An old statistical account describes the Girthgate as "a broad green path, free of the heath that grows on either side".

Plate 8: The ruins of Restlaw Ha'

Plate 9: Excavating Soutra Hospital. Reproduced courtesy of Brian Moffat.

Plate 10: Soutra Aisle before restoration. Reproduced courtesy of Brian Moffat.

# Soutra Hospital

Also between Edinburgh and the Border abbeys stood Soutra
Hospital (Plate 9). As its fame as a centre of healing spread, the
buildings grew to cope with the increasing demand and in its
heyday it became the principal hospital for the people of Edinburgh,
despite being 18 miles from the capital.

The hospital was first heard of in 1164 (but not founded then). Its
charter tells us who was eligible for care there: the poor, travellers
and pilgrims, the aged and, of course, the sick and infirm. The last
patient was recorded in 1650. All was funded from the income from
vast hospital estates mainly in the Lothians.

There are no visible buildings above ground level on the site of
the hospital today, except Soutra Aisle which was built later in 1686.
Above the door of Soutra Aisle there is a stone plaque which reads:

> THIS STONE IS INSERTED
> TO MARK THE SITE OF
> THE ANCIENT SANCTUARY
> AND ONCE POWERFUL
> HOSPICE OF SOUTRA

There was an article in *The Southern Reporter* in October 1981:

### Fight begins to save Soutra Aisle

Efforts are currently being made to trace the owner of a
derelict hospice on the windswept Soutra moors. Soutra Aisle
is the sole remnant of the once magnificent Hospital of the
Holy Trinity, reputedly founded by a charter from Malcolm IV
of Scotland in 1164.

The church itself steadily fell into disrepair following the
Reformation, and the Aisle, used as a burial chamber, is all
that now remains. Sheep currently use the building as a

shelter, and the condition of the Aisle is giving experts cause for concern. But attempts to renovate the ruin are being hindered since no one knows who the owner is.

The Aisle was restored using traditional materials in 1998 with financial help from the Lottery Fund (Plate 10, page 30).

Dr Brian Moffat has excavated some of the foundations of the hospital or hospice including what is thought to be the early 14th Century living quarters of the Augustinian Brethren and an adjoining enclosed quadrangular cloister. His investigations include the practices of medieval medicine at the hospital. He has published the results of his research in several volumes. In one volume is told the following story:

It is thought that the murder of David II's mistress, Katherine Mortimer, in 1360 took place as she was riding from Melrose near Soutra. The King, who was riding in front, returned on hearing the outcry and made great lamentation for the cruel loss.

The assassin, who was hired by certain noblemen, escaped.

Numerous writings from the Middle Ages testify to the great value ascribed to spices. Spices were, in effect, the international currency. Rents across Europe were frequently commuted into their spice equivalent, in Britain, one pound of either pepper or cumin being the commonest to be noted in collections of medieval charters. In return for the use of a piece of land near Threeburnford, between Lauderdale and the Gala Water, the Brethern of Soutra undertook to pay the Abbot and Convent of Dryburgh Abbey one pound of cumin and one pound of pepper at St James Fair, Roxburgh, each year.

In 2004, Dave Waldie ploughed up an interesting large stone

close to the hospital. On one face of the stone there is a carved pattern of concentric circles (Plate 11). The stone is yellow sandstone, which is not found locally. This type of stone is called a cup and ring stone due to its design and shape. Walter Elliot, the Border historian, thinks that the stone dates from the early Bronze Age, *ie* 2000-1500 BC, and probably came from a sun temple.

Two similar smaller stones were found in the rubble of Soutra Hospital during a dig by Brian Moffat. These stones are indeed a rare find.

A similar stone was found recently in Ancrum and is now in the Wilton Lodge Museum, Hawick.

Soutra was once called Soltref or Soltre. These words were derived from an early Welsh language, Sol meaning sun and tref meaning settlement.

Plate 11: Photograph of cup and ring stone found near Soutra Hospital

My late father recalled the following event:

> One of my earliest memories of Soutra was just before the
> First World War when I was allowed to take a trip in the
> Victoria Coach with my Grandfather. At the first Soutra gate, I
> got out and opened it, and again resumed my seat facing
> Grandpa. [They were travelling northward.]
>
> As we jolted up the ruts on the track through the heather
> further on, things were better as then there were only three
> tracks – one for the horse and two for the Victoria's wheels.
> Reaching the top of the hill where the old Aisle stands we
> were surprised to see a squad of about 20 men working on the
> road. The Irishmen had been engaged by the local authority to
> improve the road to the Aisle and so on to Gilston. (Part of the
> modern B6368, linking the A68 and A7 roads). The wall on
> the north side of the road was to a great extent composed of
> gravestones as well as field-gathered stone. The gravestones
> were being broken up as a core foundation for the road. But
> when we had come upon them, the job was almost completed,
> and much of the history of Soutra was obliterated.

I have a 25-inch to a mile Ordnance Survey map of 1965 which
shows the site of the deserted medieval village of Soutra about 64
metres (70 yards) south-east of Soutra Aisle.

On 14 June, 2006, the Visitor Centre beside Soutra Aisle was
rededicated. New laminated information boards had been provided
to replace the weather damaged ones. The information displayed
includes the following:

> At the battle of Neville's Cross in 1346, the Scots, led by David
> II, were defeated. The English border was established along
> the Lammermuir Hills from Soutra to Cockburnspath. This

would mean that for a short period of history that Soutra and
Channelkirk Parish were in England.

In modern times, the situation is like Israelis capturing the Golan
Heights from Syria for strategic reasons. The balance of power was
restored by the battle of Otterburn in 1388.

A series of beacons were erected on Scottish and English
prominent hills, and were vital as an early warning system in the
Middle Ages. Sets of one to four beacons were lit depending on the
size of the invading army. Soutra Edge is one of the key beacons
and, when it was lit "so may all Lothian be warned".

At Carter Bar on the A68 road on the Scottish-English border
stands such a beacon. Part of the inscription at its base reads: "was
part of a chain of beacons erected and lit across the United
Kingdom to mark the advent of the Single European Market. The
beacon was lit at midnight on Hogmanay (31 December) 1992.

## Dere Street

The following is from a book called *Border Highways* written by
John James Mackay:

> Dere Street continued to be used as the principal road over
> Soutra, with little or no sophisticated repairs or maintenance
> being done to the Roman work. It lasted so long because the
> amount of wheeled traffic on it was very small; most of the
> users were on foot or on horseback. It would have been quite
> unsuitable for the coaches and heavy carts being introduced in
> the 18th Century, some of the gradients being too steep for
> draught horses.
>
> Dere Street was essentially a ridgeway road when it crossed
> the hills, so avoiding the worst of the boggy areas lower down.

With a better knowledge of land drainage and river control, road designers began to see the merits of highways nearer the river basins to avoid steep gradients.

The first turnpike roads were planned from 1750 onwards. It was decided that Dere Street would have to be replaced by an easier route. This was achieved in the Turnpike Act of 1760, when the way agreed by the Trustees on both sides of the boundary was to go round the north side of Soutra Hill from the farm of the same name, on to moorland at Huntershall then to wend its way into the steep valley of the Headshaw Burn, one of the feeder streams of the Leader Water. It went by the east bank of this burn until the Leader Water was joined then followed that until Carfraemill (Plate 12).

Plate 12: Carfraemill, circa 1910. Reproduced courtesy of Robert D Clapperton, Photograghic Trust

On maps, this old road is marked as the King's Road. Today the road follows a different line, mainly due to the gradients being lessened and the road being straightened. The route of the Kings Road can still be made out from Carfraemill northward over the Soutra Plateau.

## Working mills

Carfraemill was formally called the Mill of Carfrae and also Carfrae Mill. The working Mill of Carfrae is first mentioned about 1196 and stopped grinding meal about the early 1800s. In the middle of the 18th Century wayside inns became plentiful and Carfraemill became an inn and still serves as an inn to this day. In its hey day the Inn would have had extensive stabling for horses.

Halfway down the Headshaw valley, an inn called New Channelkirk (Plate 13) had been built to serve traffic on the first

Plate 13: New Channelkirk from A68 road. The Kings Road runs along the valley floor on the far side of the farm buildings

turnpike road constructed in 1760 over Soutra. It replaced Channelkirk Inn which had been on Dere Street.

The line of the road past New Channelkirk was altered in 1835 and ran to the west close to the line of the present-day road.

In 1977, Elspeth and I and our son Malcolm went to live in New Channelkirk. At that time there were the remains of an old watermill used to thrash corn. The late Ian Sutherland remembered, as a boy, climbing inside the waterwheel and rotating it by treading the water veins. The mill wheel was driven by a series of ponds with sluice gates that were opened according to the amount of water required. This arrangement gave approximately two hours of thrashing.

One large pond was in the field to the west adjoining the steading. This was partly destroyed when the A68 road was widened and realigned in the 1980s. It would appear that the pond which lay immediately to the west of Glengelt House was also part of the system. There is evidence that there was probably another water wheel at New Channelkirk operated by the Headshaw Burn.

In 1785, just before the mailcoach, a daily passenger coach service started to Newcastle. The turnpike road over Soutra was chosen, through Greenlaw and Coldstream to Wooler and Morpeth and it proved popular. By the end of the 18th Century, the 1785 service seems to have been replaced by one going thrice-weekly all the way to London.

As the railway came to each town, so the stagecoach services ceased, leaving only the private carriages of the wealthy on the roads. They, too, disappeared quite quickly when the motorcar arrived early in the 20th Century.

# Church history

## Lauderdale's oldest church

The church at Channelkirk, the oldest one in Lauderdale, was founded between the 7th and 9th Centuries.

It has connections with the monks of Dryburgh. At Jedburgh in 1230, King Alexander II granted a general confirmation to Dryburgh Abbey of all her churches and other possessions among which is the church of Childinchurch.

Through the ages the church has been referred to as Childenchurch, Childeschirche, Childer-Kirk, Gingle-Kirk, Chingelkirk, Channonkirk and from 1716 Channelkirk. The name perhaps means "Church of the Child" after St Cuthbert.

On the church bell, which was taken down for repairs in 1990 is inscribed CHANNON KIRK 1702.

The Statistical Accounts of 1791-99 and 1845 show that the church was in the County of Berwick, Synod of Merse and Tiviotdale, and Presbytery of Lauder.

In the Statistical Account of 1885, a further explanation of the name is given as follows: "The ancient name of the parish was Childer-kirk, *ie* Childrens Kirk, having been dedicated to the Innocents. More recently its name was Gingle-kirk. It is so written in old parochial records and it is still commonly so pronounced. The origin of the name is uncertain; probably it may have had a reference to the nature of the soil, which is chiefly of a gravelly sort."

Dr Brian Moffat has found another possible derivation of the name.

Sir Robert Sibbald, Scotland's first Geographer Royal in the reign of Charles I calls the parish "Seeing-hill-kirk" after the "Seeing-hill-cross" so called because of the bonfires which were appointed by acts of parliament recorded in *Regiam Majestatum*.

Tom Cuthell, the minister of St Cuthbert's Church in Edinburgh, recently suggested that the name Channelkirk was probably named after St Conal, a Celtic Saint.

In 1654, Blaeu's *Atlas Novus* was published in Amsterdam, with 47 printed maps of parts of Scotland based on Pont and Gordon manuscripts. These maps and their associated local history texts have recently been translated from Latin and are available to look at on the internet. In the map of Lauderdale, the spelling of Channelkirk is Chingilkirk which is different from all the other spellings. There is no text to accompany this map because Blaeu asked the Second Earl of Lauderdale to provide the text. Unfortunately the Earl was captured at the battle of Worcester and the atlas had to go to print without his contribution.

# Consecration

In 1241 the Parish of Channelkirk was granted its main Charter when the Bishop of St Andrews consecrated the church lands and building during the reign of Alexander II.

With regard to that year, it is well to note that the ecclesiastical year in Europe generally commenced on 25 March. Strictly speaking, the year of the dedication would thus be 1242.

There are many well known events in history where differences in time, date and year occurred due to countries operating on different calendars. An example of this is the Bolshevik October Revolution of 1917 which, on the calendar in Britain, took place in November of that year. Until 1918 Russia used the old Julian calendar and was 13 days behind Europe, which followed the Gregorian calendar.

There was a commemorative service in the Church on Sunday 14 June 1992 to mark the 750 years and the service was taken by Dr Leonard Small. A wall hanging was made by the ladies of the parish and depicts the history of the parish. This wall hanging can be seen inside the church.

Archibald Allan records the following in his book *The History of Channelkirk* published in 1900:

> When Bishop de Bernham, stood on the hillside intent on consecrating Channelkirk Church, and when the inhabitants of the parish wended their toilsome path upwards to take part in the religious mysteries of that day of March 1241, we scarcely pause to remember that the world was very much smaller to them than it is now to us, and that hardly any of the landmarks to which we are accustomed in history were then visible. America was unknown. No-one had heard of Australia. India was a hearsay. A few had heard of China. Sir

William Wallace and Robert the Bruce were not born.
The door being opened, the Bishop and procession entered
bearing the cross, while the chest with the saint's relics was
held before the door by the priests.

A sign of the cross the length and breadth of the floor was
then made, and the cross of the Bishop fixed in the centre of
the Church, and formulas, prayers, genuflections, chants,
litany, etc, followed. After this the Greek alphabet was
written across the floor from the left corner in the East to the
right corner in the West, and a cross made with this by the
Latin alphabet written from the East right corner to the
West left. Then followed the consecration of salt, the ashes,
holy water, the wine, and the altar.

Then beginning in the East left-hand corner, as with the
Greek alphabet, the Bishop went once round the Church

Plate 14: The 13th century watermill at Mountmill.

sprinkling the walls. This was done another twice, each time a higher sprinkling being given, till the wall-tops were reached. He enacted the same ceremony outside, chanting and defying, in the language of Scripture, the winds and waters to move the walls, till finally he sprinkled the very ridge.

## Centre of the parish

When the days of comparative peace came then the path over the hill at Channelkirk carried medieval wagons of trade passing the thatched kirk and the hill village round the kirk. This was the communal centre of the parish at that time. The village has now disappeared.

The Church would have been seen by the English host of Edward II in 1314 as they came up Lauderdale to the field of Bannockburn. The English cavalry might well have fed their horses from meal ground at Mountmill (Plate 14) whose ruin in the valley below today marks the sight of the last of the mills worked here since early in the 13th Century.

It is thought that Mountmill was originally called Monks Mill, and was the place where the monks ground the corn for the local populace.

At least 80 full-sized English armies are recorded coming this way, the most frequent invasion route into Scotland. An equivalent number of Scottish armies seem probable.

Channelkirk had dependant chapels at Glengelt and at Carfrae, but the exact sites are now unknown. Sir Henry de Mundeville built Glengelt chapel in the 13th Century. He granted an indemnity to the Dryburgh Abbey canons that Glengelt should not adversely affect the mother church of Channelkirk, and gave the abbey three acres of

Plate 15: Channelkirk Church

land, two being near to the church of Channelkirk. The chapel was still in use in 1490.

On several occasions the church was rebuilt and repaired. The church was enlarged and repaired in 1653 and 10,000 divots were used to thatch it.

## A modern church

The present church (Plate 15) dates from 1817 along with manse and garden. This date is inscribed on the bell-tower. The minister at that time, John Brown, refused to continue preaching in the previous very dilapidated church building.

In *The History of Channelkirk* Archibald Allan writes:

Worry came to Mr Brown from his glebe, his church, as well as from his stipend law cases. He wished the manse repaired

44

and enlarged. It was "built 30 years ago," he said, and 30 years at Channelkirk test the best stone-and-lime structures. By that time, 1814, Brown declares the manse "totally uninhabitable.

When 1820 comes, Brown's continued clashings with his heritors have rendered him stubborn and intractable.

They actually wish now to repair the manse. They send tradesmen to the manse for this purpose, but he refuses to let them into the house. Doubtless he expected the usual handful of lime, and a door handle here and there, and nothing adequate to clear the needs of the case. Then the heritors become injured innocents!

However, Mr Brown's militant attitude eventually paid off and the heritors agreed to build a new church, but not a new manse.

The entire parish petitioned to have the new church built, not on the present site, but nearer Oxton. The heritors have our gratitude for not removing the church from its present historical site even though it was said to be inaccessible for several months during winter. For this reason, the church services now take place in the Oxton War Memorial Hall in Oxton Village between Christmas and Easter.

In Appendix 1, there is a poem entitled *The Minister Militant* which appears to be based on John Brown. There are some personal observations at the beginning of the Appendix.

The cross on the front of the church and the sundial are probably from an older church.

Around 1820 the farmers were in a bad way, having been forced to sell everything to pay their debts. They were left with no seed corn, but John Brown came to their aid by providing them with free

Plate 16: Channelkirk Manse

seed from the glebe fields. The glebe lay in two parts, one on the
height beside the church, the other in the hollow or haugh through
which the Mountmill Burn flows. In recent years, the two church
glebes were in the vicinity of the church, but both of them have been
sold.

## Manse destroyed

James Walker, the minister at Channelkirk, resigned his charge on
11 December 1884 and he and his family emigrated to Vancouver,
British Columbia. On the occasion of the departure, the manse was
completely destroyed by fire. The silver communion cups were lost
in the catastrophe, and police from Edinburgh could find no trace of
the melted silver. A new manse (Plate 16) was built to replace the
old one and still stands next to the church. There is still some
evidence of the previous manse. There is a story told locally that Mr

Walker left his wife and family destitute and emigrated to Vancouver with a girl half his age who used to work in the manse. The manse was sold for private occupation in 1926.

It was not the only fire at the manse as *The Southern Reporter* of September 1939 records:

### Oxton Fire

Galashiels Brigade Fight Flames

A fire occurred at "Lindores" formally "Old Channelkirk Manse". It was confined to the outhouses, adjoining the Manse. These were gutted. The fire was thought to be caused by the bursting of a primus stove.

Galashiels Fire Brigade arrived at the scene of the fire within half an hour. The manse buildings were saved by the energies of the locals and the Fire Brigade who led their hose to the Leader, a distance of approximately 300 yards (274 metres), and there got a good volume of water. The real danger was that there were 5 tons of coals which if they had got right alight would have probably ignited the manse itself.

The manse was the property of Captain Stewart. Mrs Stewart had an alarming time. She was ill in bed, and the only other person in the manse was the housekeeper.

After Captain and Mrs Stewart, the Mackays lived in Lindores, now called Channelkirk House. Drew Kellet from Lauder remembers that he was taught geography in the late 1950s by Mrs Mackay at Earlston Junior Secondary School.

## Kirk House

After the manse was sold for private occupation in 1926, a new manse was built in Oxton village. This building is now called

Plate 17: Kirk House

Kirk House (Plate 17). The last minister to live in the new Channelkirk manse was Francis Fordyce, who was a retired minister. He lived in the manse with his sister and preached in the church on Sunday, but did not perform any other duties. A congregational meeting was held in January 1973, when it was decided to link with Lauder Old. The Channelkirk manse was then sold and Mr James became the minister.

In the early 1900s the remains of a steading were still visible in the glebe to the north of the church. These were the ruins of Channelkirk Farm.

*The Scotsman* published this article in July 1938:

CHANNELKIRK. – A sale of work organised by the Woman's Guild of Channelkirk Parish Church was held in the War Memorial Hall, Oxton, when a sum of £97 was realised. The sale was opened by Mrs McConnachie, of Lauder, at whose suggestion a telegram was sent to His

Majesty the King – "The Woman's Guild of Channelkirk
Parish Church desire to express the wish that Your Majesty
may be strengthened by your sojourn in France and Her
Majesty may have a happy visit."

The following reply was received: "Please convey to the Woman's
Guild of Channelkirk Parish Church assembled this evening the
sincere thanks of the King and Queen for their kind message of
good wishes. My wife's maiden name was also MacConachie (spelt a
different way).

The late Ernie Miller on his last day at work before retiring as the
local roadman uncovered the old horse trough at the bend of the
road opposite the Old Manse. There used to be a mug there for
people to drink from when they came toiling up the slope from
Oxton to go to church.

The church bell was taken down and a crack in it was repaired
about 1990. At the same time part of the graveyard wall was rebuilt.
The wall is approximately 1.7 metres in height and has contributed
to shielding the gravestones from weather damage.

## Sessions unite

In June 2005, the Kirk Sessions of Channelkirk and Lauder united
into one Session.

The last minister of the parishes of Channelkirk and Lauder, the
Rev John Shields, retired in July 2007 and it seems likely that these
parishes will be merged with at least one of the surrounding
parishes. John and his wife, Mary, have retired to the Kelso area and
will be sorely missed by their many friends.

At the present time there is an interim minister and services
continue as before.

# Some Ministers and their Times

Was St Cuthbert the first minister of the gospel at Channelkirk? We
may never know the answer, but it is believed that it was on the
slopes of Channelkirk that he had his vision of St Aidan being carried
up to heaven by a host of angels. It was, of course, a long time ago,
and other areas lay claim to the saint. But what we do know for
certain is that the following churchmen did preach at Channelkirk:

## Ninian Borthwick, 1567 to 1576

It is seven years after the Reformation, and the desolation of the
Church is still evident. When the priests were cut adrift, many
churches were left without any person of sufficient status and
ordination to conduct divine services for the people. Here Ninian
Borthwick not only officiates in his own parish of Lauder, but also
has Channelkirk under his care.

## Henry Cockburn, 1625 to 1650

One of the early acts of Charles I was to was to ride up with his followers and present the new minister to Channelkirk on 4 July, 1625.

The minister had no manse, the Church half in ruins, hardly any glebe, though the church of Channelkirk had abounded in possession of acres, not even a bit of wide wild moor of Soutra to cast peats in, or lift a divit out of, and the stipend of £27 - 15s - 6 8/12d on which to support 10 people. No wonder the minister could not entertain anyone. He must have been on the brink of starvation. Four hundred communicants were gathering in a church with half its roof off. The stipend came from Glengelt, Kirktonhill and Headshaw. Henry Cockburn was deposed for praying for the English army under the Duke of Hamilton in 1650. He was reinstated again in 1662.

Cromwell's soldiers took up residence at Thirlestane about July 1649 and kept the country for miles around in a state of panic. They raided the poor box at Channelkirk.

Borthwick Castle near Middleton held out against his forces. The evidence of the damage done by the cannon balls is still there. My brother has the letter signed by Cromwell with his wax seal asking Lord John Borthwick and his men to surrender, which they did and were allowed to march out with honour as free men. By coincidence, Cromwell's Paymaster General was another ancestor, Sir John Borthwick.

## David Liddell, 1650 to 1662

If Henry Cockburn has a strong claim to be the martyr of Channelkirk, his successor David Liddell has an undoubted title to be called our Scholar.

CHAPTER 3

He is most probably related to the family of Liddells who were benefactors of and professors in Marischal College in Aberdeen in the 17th Century. His first appearance at Channelkirk is in the memorable year of 1650 which saw, among other notable events, the Psalms first put into metrical form by Francis Rous, and the Marquis of Montrose executed in Edinburgh. A story from the *History of Channelkirk* illustrates the times that the minister lived in:

> Conspicuous over all, watchful, fierce, and despotic, towers the Kirk session. None escapes its vigilance, as few are able to elude its ban. Peer or peasant, farmer or hind, rich or poor, all must bow to its dictates and listen to its commands. It was an almonry for the poor and needy.
> And it is not only in the church where its power is felt. Not a pailful of water can be carried home from the well, but cognisance is taken whether it is done on Sabbath or Saturday. So with carrying food, or yoking a cart.
> Not a fiddle may twangle at marriage or merrymaking beyond the hours and bounds fixed by this small body. Fathers of families are roundly told in what ways they should bear themselves at home or afield. The weakest and most weather-winnowed creature in the parish, it may be, when once seated in the chair of the elder, does not hesitate to fulminate his judgements with a "Thus saith the Lord."

These are features of Scottish life which, of course, were perfectly general over the country. None disputed the minister's authority; all except the most profane and hardened meekly yielded place to him.

David Liddell left Channelkirk in 1674 and was elected by unanimous consent and common vote of all the moderators, Professor of Theology in Glasgow University.

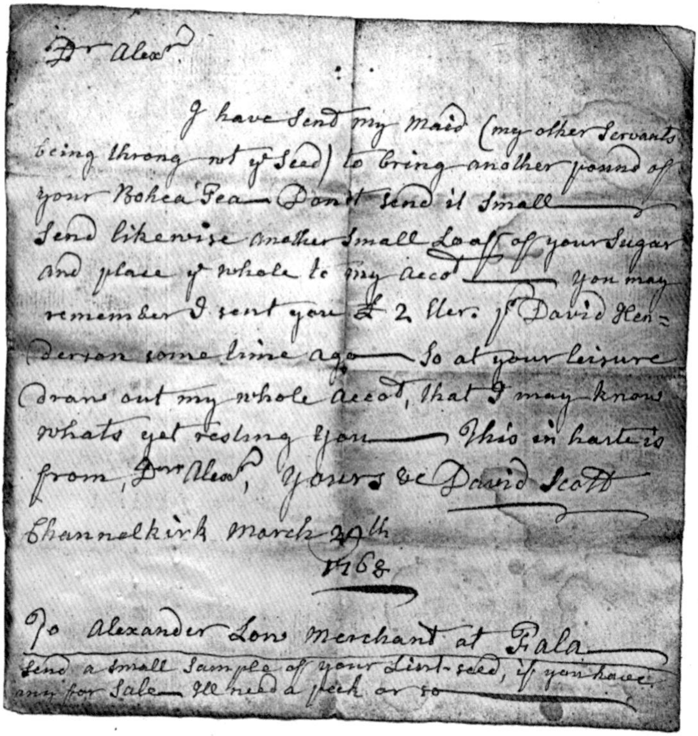

Plate 18: Letter written in 1768 by David Scott, minister at Channelkirk to
Alexander Low, merchant at Fala. Reproduced courtesy of Lindsay Errington

## David Scott, 1751 to 1792

I would like to quote from a letter of 1768 in which a gentleman
living at Channelkirk is requesting provisions from a trader called
Alexander Low in Fala (Plate 18).

> I have sent my maid (my other servants being throng at ye
> seed) to bring another pound of your Bohea tea – don't send
> it small – send likewise another small loaf of your sugar and
> place ye whole to my account – you may remember I sent
> you £2 sterling by David Henderson some time ago – so at

54

your leasure draw out my whole account that I may know
what yet's resting you – This in haste is from, Dear
Alexander, Yours etc David Scott,
Channelkirk March 1768.
To Alexander Low Merchant at Fala.
Send a small sample of your Lint-seed, if you have any for
sale – I'll need a peck or so.

Lint seed was for growing a plant from which linen yarn was
made. A peck was about two gallons liquid or dry weight. Bohea tea
was black tea which was a high class drink. Normally people drank
green herbal tea, as they still do in many parts of the world today.

I am indebted to Lindsay Errington for a copy of this letter and
further information about Alexander Low. Lindsay found this letter
wedged between the rafters when she moved into No 3 Fala.
Alexander Low also lived at No 3 Fala, and was buried in Humbie
churchyard. Blackshiels was actually part of Humbie parish not
Fala, in those days.

This letter must have been written by an educated man and on
investigation it turns out to be David Scott, the minister at
Channelkirk between 1751 and 1792.

## James Rutherford 1828 to 1862

Archibald Allan describes him as a man who "shrank from publicity
in every form and was rather shy than otherwise in the social
relationships of the church". He preferred to spend his forenoons
alone in the church rather than in the domestic bustle of the manse.
During his tenure of office a national fast day was held in March
1832 and 1849 on account of the cholera epidemics then raging.

The Disruption of 1843 led to the resignation of the schoolmaster who, together with one of the elders, adhered to the Free Church. At this time Patronage was the accepted method of appointing ministers. They were not, as today, chosen by their congregations but were "presented" to them by the "Patron of the Living", who might be the bishop, a landowner, or a group of landowners in the parish known as Heritors. A "Patron of the Living" could also be the Crown as witnessed by the congregation of Channelkirk in 1625, when Charles I rode up to present the new minister.

In 1843 after years of debate in the General Assembly, the issue of Patronage brought another division, the Disruption. Over one third of the ministers of the Church, along with large numbers of their congregations, left the Church of Scotland and formed the Free Church of Scotland. In 1900, The Free Church resolved on union with the United Presbyterian Church and the resulting United Free Church came back into the Church of Scotland in the Union of 1929.

A portrait of Mr Rutherford was retrieved from the belfry of Stow Parish Church in 1996, refurbished, and placed in the vestry in Channelkirk Church.

The Rev James Rutherford wrote the Statistical Account of 1845 for the Parish and this is available on the internet, together with the Statistical Account of 1791-99 written by the Rev Thomas Murray.

Thomas Murray wrote in his account: "The chief advantage of our situation is the contiguity to the public road which leads from Edinburgh to London. It is kept in excellent repair by the money collected at the toll bars."

## Archibald Allan, 1891 to 1924

Archibald Allan was a scholar and wrote the *History of Channelkirk,* published in 1900, which has been the source of much information for this book. He had a princely form and bearing, for he was over 6ft in stature, and had the features of George the Fourth. He is buried at the door of the church together with his wife and daughter. His daughter was buried in 1984 and is the last person to be buried in the Channelkirk graveyard.

There is a paragraph at the end of his book which reads:

> Nothing has transpired in the valley for centuries to equal in importance, perhaps, the advent of the railway. The situation of Lauderdale cuts it off from all communication with the outside world, except that is afforded across Soutra Hill on the north and Stow hills on the west. In winter this means, in too many instances, no communication at all, owing to the roads being blocked with snow. This season proved the express need of a change in the distressing inconveniences which the long-continued storm produced.
>
> On 9th December of last year 1899, a south-east wind, accompanied with frost, set in, which increased in severity till on the 11th and 12th snow was obstructively lying everywhere. Scarcely any change took place till the latter days of March, February having been the wildest month of snowstorms within living memory.

This paragraph seemed particularly apt, as on the night of Monday 26 February until the night of Tuesday 27 February 2001 a snow storm came from the north-east and closed all communications in Lauderdale and the Borders (Plate 19, page 58). Most farmers cannot remember a storm with such ferocity. A large number of sheep were buried and those that were not rescued in time perished. Many of these were heavy with lamb. The road over Soutra was closed for two-and-a-half days and most subsidiary roads took four to six days to clear.

The road past Channelkirk Church leading to Kirktonhill was cleared by Billy Steele using his JCB on Saturday 3 March, two other attempts by JCB's having failed. The piles of snow at the side of the road reach approximately 10 ft in places (Plate 20).

Electricity had been restored to most of Oxton including Channelkirk on Thursday 1 March. The A697 road from Carfraemill to Greenlaw was only opened on Sunday 4 March. Prime Minister Tony Blair informed us on a radio broadcast that it was the worst storm in this part of Scotland for 40 years.

After this story about the snow, in the summer of 2003, Channelkirk House and Channelkirk Cottage ran out of water for about six weeks when our spring dried up. We have had a borehole sunk, which now supplies our water.

Parish records between 1892 and 1899 show that the number of

Plate 19: Picture of Oxton Village, February 2001

CHAPTER 3

Plate 20: Channelkirk Cottage in foreground and Church in background,
February 2001

people on the church roll varied between 142 and 217. These figures
are higher than the church roll in recent years.

An obituary for the Rev Archibald Allan appeared in *The Scotsman*
in November 1924. The obituary is edited due to its length:

> Sir, –The brief obituary reference in your columns today to
> the minister of Channelkirk should be supplemented. Mr
> Allan was a remarkable man. Originally a coal-pit boy, he
> was early filled with the ambition to find a higher niche in
> life. His way to the university was only reached after hard
> toil and sacrifice. He had a passion for music, and an
> unrivalled knowledge of the violin, which instrument he
> taught at nights to the rustics of his native Fife.
> He did well at St Andrews, was licensed, became assistant at

Ladhope, Galashiels and, finally, minister of a parish which embraced the furthest bounds of Lauderdale. There he laboured from 1891 to 1924.

He was an able preacher, a born raconteur, a lovable companion, a kindly pastor, and friend. He was the historian of his parish.

His *History of Channelkirk* is a monument of careful and erudite research, in which the author went to every available original source for his facts, not content to accept the gleanings of others or the data of already printed collections, as is so often the case with the local analyst. He was an accomplished and advanced theologian, as is evidenced by his volumes, *The Advent of the Father* and *The Transfiguration*, both solid and serious contributions to Christological literature.

Mr Allan never courted the limelight. He preferred the company of his books, and the solace of his own studies, and was pleased to minister to a handful of farmers, shepherds, and country folk, who probably did not realise the treasure they had in their midst. One has often wondered why this man did not receive some mark of distinction from his own or another university.

Others infinitely less scholarly, infinitely less deserving, have been able somehow to achieve such honours, but the humble, unassuming scholar of Channelkirk was apparently forgotten! – I am, &c.

John Lauderdale.

The obituary also mentioned that he had completed a book on metaphysics, a volume of verse, and had started his autobiography.

# Richard James 1973 to 1982

Mr James wrote a book called *Lauder – Its Kirk and People*. He was a kind and scholarly man. Under his guardianship, Channelkirk was again linked with Lauder.

During the time Mr James was minister, the church was painted the present colour of pink/terracotta. Prior to this event it was grey and difficult to pick out from its surroundings.

Mr James lived in the manse in Lauder which was sold after he retired. It was a large building and in need of a lot of repair. Just before he retired the manse was struck by lightening.

When Elspeth, Malcolm and I came to Channelkirk in 1977, the church had a thriving Sunday School with over 20 children attending. It took place in the Oxton Memorial Hall on a Sunday morning and included hymn singing, stories and play-acting. The highlight of the Sunday School was, at the start, when the children eagerly gave their news from the past week. There were some surprises here! A group of ladies from the village and farmers wives all gave of their time willingly.

At the end of the year, Bibles were presented to the children for good attendance by the minister. There were Sunday School outings and one of the highlights of the year was performing in the Nativity play at the Christmas Eve midnight carol service. Hardly a space was to be had in the church. There was great anticipation as the first act of the play was about to start and the only light in the church was on the stage. After the service, most of the children rushed home with great excitement to open their Christmas presents.

The following is a quote from John Mackay's article in *The Scots Magazine* of January 1982:

> Another memory for us former town dwellers: Airhouse farm in a Christmas glow – as with other hospitable farms in the

following years – the children ready for bed but still lively, having recently come from the Nativity play in the kirk where the not long established electric was ignored and folk came into the building with lantern or torch, making strange shadow patterns on the ceiling, before settling down to listen to the age old story in the unaffected Border's tongue. Outside again, a slow skailin of the kirk; then, after the last car lights had gone twisting down the brae, a minute just to stand on the now empty roadway to look north to Soutra's edge, black against the faint glow from Lothian. Distant car lights moving north and south like fireflies marked the line of the A68; and left, the nearer dark wood of Kirktonhill marked the line of Dere Street – the Roman way – and the way for so many more in Scotland's story.

# Channelkirk graves

Graves face East to West as is Christian custom. When Adam and Eve were expelled from the Garden of Eden an angel was placed at the east gate to prevent them returning – that means that Eden was to the west of where they were living. They hoped some day to return to Eden so they faced Eden after death, *ie* head end of the body is to the west pointing west.

## Gravestones in Channelkirk Churchyard

The gravestones (Plate 21, page 64) have a range of interesting symbols engraved on them. Some of them are:

> Wings with head or skull – departure of the spirit.
>
> Implements carved on gravestone – representing craft.
>
> Skull and crossbones – ancient Masonic sign or symbol for plague or disease or used to scare grave robbers.
>
> Hourglass on its side – representing time standing still between present time and coming time.
>
> Table stone gravestone – to stop grave robbers.

Plate 21: View of Channelkirk Church and graveyard looking at southwest corner of church. Reproduced courtesy of the *Southern Reporter*

Writing on the gravestones is on the east side of the stones – perhaps due to the prevailing wind weathering the stones.

The name of Ugston on older gravestones is the old name for Oxton. The name change occurred about 1837.

## Mort safe

Against the wall at the north of the church there used to be is a mort safe. It is being restored. The bodies of two children were snatched from Channelkirk graveyard and their bodies were left in the Bairns Cundie or Bairns Conduit as it is marked on an old map. The villagers reburied them, but failed to catch the robbers when they returned to pick up the bodies. The Bairns Cundie lies further up from Glengelt on the left side of the A68 going north, just at the lay-by. Unfortunately it was partly filled in when the road was widened in the 1980s.

## War memorials

In 1945 an RAF plane crashed into the Windy Cleugh which lies just up from the Cundie on Turf Law. The plane hit the wood and crashed into the hillside ending up in the cleugh. The wood was felled in the late 1940s and only the moss-covered tree stumps remain. David Lees, the shepherd at the Den, found the crashed plane, and asked a passing motorist to report the crash to the Police Station at Lauder. John Gilchrist remembers when he was young, picking up fragments of perspex at the crash site.

The plane, which was an Avro Anson, Identification No NK 945, took off from Kinloss in Morayshire on Wednesday 7 February, 1945 bound for Castle Bromwich near Birmingham. On board the plane were a pilot, an observer and passenger/second pilot. While flying over the Borders the plane encountered a snowstorm and turned back and crashed on Turf Law with no survivors. The passenger, Vaclav Jicha, was Czechoslovakian and holder of the DFC and AFC. He is buried in the RC Cemetery in Haddington.

In 1999 a car drew up in Oxton with a number of ladies from Haddington. With them was an elderly Czechoslovakian lady. They asked where the aeroplane had crashed on Turf Law. It turned out that the Czechoslovakian lady was making a pilgrimage to see where her fiancé had crashed.

Since then, Vaclav's fiancé, Juliette Liuska, has made regular visits to his grave. A member of the Spitfire Association, hearing about this, readily agreed to have a Spitfire fly to Haddington. In September 2007, as Juliette tended Vaclav's grave, a Spitfire appeared and made three passes above her and on the last, dipped its wings in salute before flying back to Leuchars in Fife.

Inside the church there is a plaque commemorating the fallen of the First and Second World War and also a plaque containing the names of the present and former ministers of Channelkirk. There is a soldier buried in the graveyard who is not on the role.

## Graves on south side of church

Plate 22: Grave of shepherd and his dog in Channelkirk graveyard at SW corner of church

The oldest discernable writing on any of the graves is from the time
of Charles I. It is on a flat stone behind the pulpit: 1642 George
Sommerville of Airhouse.

On a small stone, erected to the memory of Mary Beattie who died
at Glengelt 29th March 1886 aged 9 years and 6 months is a poem:

> Let my sins be all forgiven
> Bless the friends I love so well
> Take me when I die to heaven
> Happy there with thee to dwell

## South-west of the church

Placed against the corner of the church (Plate 22):

> James Waterston died 1781
> Shepherd and dog lost in snowstorm on Headshaw. There is
> a carving of shepherd, with his dog at the bottom of the
> gravestone.

Gravestone lying down:

> Here lies John Dewer, husband of Elspeth Stewart who departed
> this life 21st March 1685 being the 65th year of his age.

There is an hour glass and a skull and crossbones and on the
other side of the gravestone are wings and head and a poem:

> Here lyeth my bones
> now free from groans
> waiting the spring
> my soul is above
> with Christ in love
> and there doth ring

Adam Walker died at Friar's Nose in 1886. He was going to be
buried at Stow, but was diverted in a snowstorm to Channelkirk.

Plate 23: Grave of Marian Brock

# North-west of church

Carved stone with writing facing outside wall (Plate 23).

> Here lyeth Marion Brock
>
> daughter to William Brock
>
> Gardener in Ugston who departed the 29th April 1721
>
> and her age 19 years.

It has a rake and spade on the gravestone and the inscription on the grave is in old English.

# East of church

Henry Marshall Liddell died 1921

for 28 years Headmaster of the Parish. Inspector of the Poor.

Heritors Clerk and Registrar.

He laboured for the good of the community.

# Outside the church

Archibald Allan's grave is on the old footpath to the church (Plate 24). Mr Allan said that as people walked over him in life, they could walk over him in death. Parishioners now arrive by car, park in the new car park, and enter the church from a different direction.

Plate 24: Grave of Archibald Allen at the Church door. The grave (left) is enclosed by a low railing

Archibald Allan, who wrote the *History of Channelkirk*, was minister for 33 years. He died in 1924.

John Gilchrist recalled that during the snow storms in early 1947 Dod Bell, who drove horses at Burnfoot, died. Burnfoot lies 0.8 km (0.5 mile) south-east from Oxton. The roads were all blocked with snow. The brae up to the kirk had been hand cast with shovels, but had blown full again. The funeral was arranged and a pair of horses from Kirktonhill set out with a sledge to take the coffin to the kirk yard. The horses got stuck between Mountmill and Braefoot and had to turn back. Dod Scott accompanied the horses back and John Burrell went on to alert the people at Burnfoot.

Will Hume managed to take the coffin, with his horse and sledge, through the fields to Oxton. The horses were changed and the coffin taken by John Gilchrist up the A68 road and up the Mid Park field to the top. Then the coffin was carried to the graveside. John omitted his own name, when he told me the story, but I have put it in. This was all in a fierce snow storm. Most of the mourners stood on the wall of the kirk yard for safety due to the depth of the snow.

Dod Bell used to deliver coal to Oxton including taking his horse and cart up and down The Row (see plates 34 and 43, Chapter 7).

In 1947, a horse and sledge generally provided the only means of transport about the farms in snowy weather and was vital for feeding sheep and cattle in the fields. In the late 1940s horses started to be replaced by tractors.

The old graveyard at Channelkirk is long since full and a new one on the outskirts of Oxton has now been in use since 1933.

# Sower's burial plaque

There are instances when people were not buried in either Channelkirk Graveyard or the graveyard near Oxton, but somewhere else locally.

In 1734 there was a sower sowing his beans at Threeburnford on a Sunday. He was killed by lightening before his beans could be harvested and was not allowed to be buried in the churchyard. There is a plaque to him in the wall of the steading at Threeburnford (Plate 25). Perhaps the saying "It is not worth a row of beans" is significant here.

In Appendix 2, there is a poem entitled *A Lammermoor Legend* which is written about this incident. There are some personal observations at the beginning of the Appendix.

Plate 25: The plaque to the Sower in the wall of the steading at Threeburnford

In the year 2000, John Bartlett, who was a humanist, was buried at a spot above Carfrae Farm steading looking across the valley to the church and the Oxton graveyard.

In history, there have been many sad epitaphs on gravestones, perhaps none sadder than Robert III, great grandson of Robert the Bruce, who spoke his own epitaph: "Here lies the worst of kings and the most miserable of men." 4 April 1406.

# Upper Lauderdale and the Soutra Plateau

## Channelkirk Cottage

It is thought that the oldest part of Channelkirk Cottage (Map 2, page 14), which lies about 150 metres above the Church, is the last remaining part of the old village of Channelkirk. This is where my wife, Elspeth, and I have lived since 1983. It appears that the cottage originally was a "one up and one down" with an outside stair.

In 1975, Ann Longden lived in Channelkirk Cottage. During the Christmas period, the snow was deep and the cold severe. On returning from work, she lit the fire in the sitting room. Her Labrador cross Irish Wolfhound was comfortably resting on the sofa opposite the fire. The water in the back boiler was frozen which caused an explosion, sending the grate of the fire across the room, narrowly missing the dog, and through the partition wall into the kitchen, leaving a large charred hole in the wall.

The explosion was so severe that the whole gable end of the house was left with a bulge. Luckily, Miss Longden was standing to one side when the explosion happened but, even so, she was badly scalded and burned. The dog escaped harm, but one of her two cats was also badly scalded and burned. Worse was to come as the carpet and furnishings of the sitting room caught fire and, with great difficulty, Miss Longden put out the fire. She called a doctor and the fire service but neither could attend due to the depth of snow. The cat eventually recovered from its wounds.

The following spring, when the cottage was being repaired, Ian Landells from Lauder recalled the following event: "The builder had just finished repairing the outside of the house and I was finishing putting the plaster board in place in the kitchen when I heard a cheeping sound. On removing the sheet of plasterboard, I discovered a nest of baby birds." A passageway was left for the Pied Wagtail to continue feeding her young.

The Scott family lived in Channelkirk Cottage for many years. Willie was the shepherd at Kirktonhill. When we moved in to Channelkirk Cottage we cut down a decaying ash tree in the garden and it had a coil of wire on one of the branches. This was to hang a pig after it had been killed. There is still the remains of the pigsty in the wood behind the cottage, its walls constructed from railway sleepers from the former Lauder Light Railway which passed through the valley below. In those days it was common practice to keep a pig and some hens to supplement both diet and income.

Mrs Scott recalls that one winter when the snow was very deep, the only way out of the house was through the bathroom window.

The size and location of the window must have made this a difficult operation.

The Rev Archibald Allan records the following events, which took place in 1745:

> "On the north side of the road adjoining the manse stood the inn where Sir John Cope breakfasted on the morning of his defeat at Prestonpans, and where Prince Charlie's soldiers refreshed themselves".

The inn was latterly reffered to as Old Channelkirk Inn to distinguish it from New Channelkirk.

After the battle, General Sir John Cope went on to spend the night in Lauder.

In the words of the song *Johnnie Cope:*

> Cope sent a letter from Dunbar,
> saying Charlie meet me if ye daur,
> And I'll learn you the art o' war,
> If you'll meet me in the morning.

It was one of the bloodiest but briefest encounters in the history of East Lothian, when the government forces finally caught up with the Jacobite army of Bonnie Prince Charlie. More than 300 men from both sides died. The earliest known wagon-way was the Tranent-Cockenzie wagon-way which was commandeered by the Jacobites and used to transport cannon. This was the first recorded use of a railway for military purposes in this country. The Young Pretender allowed the Jacobites to build up their strength in Edinburgh ahead of their march into England.

When Bonnie Prince Charlie's troops left Edinburgh on their way south to Kelso, the prince slept at Thirlestane, but his Highlanders were billeted at the farms on the ridge round Channelkirk. A few of his Highlanders took the opportunity to desert and return home.

Some evidence of the clansmen still remain. Colonel and Mrs Murray found a Highland dirkfork while digging in their garden at Heriotshiels on the outskirts of Oxton.

# Fire and quakes

About 700 metres across the fields from the church and manse lies the farm steading of Kirktonhill, destroyed by fire in 1958. The steading contained a stationery threshing mill driven by an oil engine. Each bearing on the oil engine was drip lubricated from an oil can and the waste oil splattered on the floor. A blow lamp was used to warm the cylinder head of the engine prior to starting. On this occasion, the blow lamp tipped over and set fire to the waste oil, which soon set fire to the straw. Despite the best efforts of the people working on the farm and the fire brigade, only the damaged stone walls of the steading remained.

In *The Scotsman* of 28 March 1938, the following item appeared:

> **The Earth Tremor**
>
> Channelkirk, Oxton, March 26, 1938
>
> Sir, - It may interest readers to know that the earth tremor reported to have been experienced in Edinburgh on Monday night was distinctly heard and felt here in Channelkirk, Oxton. I was awake at the time and heard a low distant rumble; then the room seemed to shudder! On the following morning I mentioned my experience, but no one had felt anything unusual. It was therefore a little satisfaction to my mind to read in the *Scotsman* that there had been a shock, and that I had not been dreaming. I am &c
>
> (Mrs) MW Stewart.

On Christmas Eve 1979 there was also an earth tremor. Elspeth experienced the tremor, but nobody else in the house felt it. Other people in the area also experienced it. An arrangement of flowers fell off the mantelpiece at Hartside and a wall cracked in the steading at Kirktonhill.

## New Channelkirk

When Elspeth and I lived at New Channelkirk we used to get tramps coming down to the farm. They usually got some hot soup, sandwiches and a warm place to sleep in the straw barn. They generally left the next morning to continue their journey. This happened until the 1980s, when their way of life must have changed. There is a story told locally of a tramp who pushed a pram containing his possessions along the highways and byways. He had a PhD in chemistry, but had decided to drop out of society.

New Channelkirk is easily seen in the valley below from the A 68 road. People involved in or witnessing road accidents would come down for help. Elspeth's nursing training was often put to good use. One man came down after having had an alarming experience. While driving down the road, the cab of his lorry tilted forward and the lorry skidded, with his face close to the road, for some distance before coming to a halt. The man was in a state of shock and was cut and bruised. He also had fragments of glass in his eye which were removed by Dr Harry Crombie Smith in Lauder.

The late Dr Harry Crombie Smith remembered when there used to be a road for vehicles from Kirktonhill to New Channelkirk which crossed the main A68 road. At the point of crossing on the west side of the A68 stood the Channelkirk Cottages. These were two semi-detached cottages occupied until the 1960s (centre distance, Plate 26, page 78). The late Dr Mary Sutherland remembered delivering a baby in one of the cottages. They became derelict and were finally demolished in the 1980s.

Plate 26: Looking down Upper Lauderdale, January 1979. Blue-grey cows are on the left with New Channelkirk behind and Channelkirk Cottages in the centre distance. Glengelt lies to the right of the trees in the foreground. Reproduced courtesy of John Wilkie

Plate 27: Glengelt House. The Soutra Plateau runs along the skyline

Also in Plate 26 are some Blue-grey cows which I used to feed every morning in the winter months. This breed of cow is now rare and most farmers have continental (European) breeds of cattle.

## Borthwick connections

The Borthwicks have been associated with Channelkirk for a long time. In the year 1458 at Edinburgh, King James II gave to Lord William Borthwick and his heirs the lands of Glengelt in Berwickshire, which Mary Pringle in her widowhood had resigned. Lord William married her in the same year.

Sir William Borthwick, father of this Lord William of Glengelt, was Ambassador to Rome in 1425, and was created the first Lord Borthwick in 1433.

## Coal

There is a paragraph taken from the 1983 Yearbook of the Gorebridge & District Local History Society which reads:

"It is not known when coal was first dug at Stobs or Newbyres (in the area which is now Gorebridge). The monks of Newbattle may have had workings before 1543, the year in which they sold Newbyres to the Borthwicks of Glengelt. But even when Michael Borthwick obtained a licence from Parliament to dig a day level to drain the coal workings at Newbyres in 1582, it was clearly a very small-scale operation."

Sir James Dundas of Arniston bought Newbyres in 1624 and the castle which the Borthwicks had built became used as the Arniston dower-house. The castle is called Newbyres Castle and its remains can still be seen.

There is a carved stone plaque at the back of Glengelt House with the inscription "Agnes Hunter 1742". This indicates Agnes Hunter married a Borthwick and the lands of Glengelt and Hunters Hall were united.

There is evidence that Glengelt House (Plate 27) once had an ingleneuk fireplace.

Recently I found a *Scotsman* newspaper cutting of May 1937 which contained the obituary of my grandfather, Henry Borthwick. It included the following paragraph:

> Mr Borthwick was laird of Glengelt, holding this grant of land direct from the Crown. A condition is that the owner should present a white rose to the Royal Sovereign when he passed that way, and this condition has been honoured on several occasions. Once the train conveying Queen Victoria was stopped at Fountainhall Station in order that Mr Borthwick's predecessor should present a bouquet of roses.

## Hunters Hall

Known locally as the Den or Lourie's Den, Hunters Hall lies adjacent to the A68 on top of Soutra. The present building was formerly an inn and then a shepherd's house until about 1979 and now lies derelict. From statistical records the following is recorded: "Hunters Hall formally an inn is the highest inhabited house in the country at 1,093 feet."

Quoting from Archibald Allan's *History of Channelkirk:*

> A person of the name of Lourie was said to have been the innkeeper in old times, and hence its name of Lourie's Den. It was once the great stopping place for drovers' carts and carriers from Lauderdale and the south, going to and from Dalkeith market and other places north.
> Lourie's Den had a sinister reputation. Several packmen or peddlers had mysteriously disappeared. No clue to their fate was got until one warm summer, many years after, the goose-dub or small pond opposite the door became completely dry

and exposed a number of human bones, revealing the gruesome secret.

There is a story told locally that Lourie murdered his wife and bricked up her remains within Lourie's Den. Several people who have slept there have testified to hearing a tapping sound. Although the building has been searched from top to bottom, the source of the tapping cannot be found.

It is said that Prince Charlie's highlanders, on the march to England, stopped and got refreshments there. At one time, a bloody fight between two gypsies of the Faa and Shaw tribes took place in the field opposite the inn, when one of them was killed.

The survivor was tried and hanged. It is also recorded in 1679 that there was a battle between the two same Gypsy tribes at Romano Bridge.

## Gypsy battles

There is a story about the Faa tribe told in *Wilson's tales of the Borders* which begins:

> You have all heard of the celebrated Johnny Faa, the Lord and Earl of Little Egypt, who penetrated into Scotland in the reign of James IV, and with whom that gallant monarch was glad to conclude a treaty.
>
> Johnny was not only the king, but the first of the Faa gang of whom we have mention, and though it is difficult to account for the name satisfactorily, it is said to have had its origin from a family of the name of Fall or Fa', who resided in Rothbury, and that their superiority in their cunning and desperate profession gave the same cognomen to all and sundry who followed the same mode of life upon the Borders.

With reference to "Little Egypt" mentioned above, the gypsies were once thought to have come from Egypt and the name Gypsy is derived from Egyptian. In 1892, the last Gypsy king, Charles Faa-Blyth was crowned at Kirk Yetholm. Now only a handful of Gypsy families remain.

For many years the gypsies had used the Kings Inch on Soutra as a halting place in their travels round the country. The Kings Inch is situated 1.2 km (0.75 mile) south of Soutra Aisle beside the River Armet. It is situated on the Girthgate. At this point, Dere Street has merged with the Girthgate and they have become a common road over the northern part of the Soutra Plateau.

Every year, there is a fair on the green at St Boswells which is always held on 18 July, the saint's day of Boisil. The earliest mention of this Gypsy event is in 1621 and was originally a sheep fair.

## Whisky in the moss

Stories and legends of the area have been recorded in many places. The following was published in *The Scots Magazine* of February 1977 and written by John Mackay:

> Headshaw Moss is on our left going south as the A68 leaves the moorland plateau of Soutra. The road twists as it begins its descent, disclosing the first glimpse of the Dale of the Leader – Lauderdale – with the Black Hill at Earlston to the left, two of the triple peaks of Eildon distant right, and the blue line of the Cheviots on the far horizon.
>
> A story about Headshaw Moss was told to me by Bob Young of Oxton:"There's an auld cottage out on Carfrae Common," he said, "and there was once a herd (shepherd) in it who used to make his own whisky. This was a long time ago when the cart road was ower the hill top. Well, one misty

day the Excisemen came across the hill to catch him, and met another herd and asked him the way to the cottage. He guessed what they were after so he sent them a roundabout road and then took a short cut himself to the whisky herd's place. The two herds took the barrel o' whisky that had been new casked and they rolled it down the hill into Headshaw Moss. It was an auld herd who told that story to my Uncle John when he was at Fairnylees. Right up to the 1930s the pair o' them would whiles go down to the Moss and prod away with their crooks – but they never found the barrel."

## Lost in bog

During World War Two, in the vicinity of Headshaw Moss, a light armoured vehicle got sucked into the bog while on a military training exercise.

## Midside Maggie

John Mackay went on in *The Scots Magazine* article to recount the tale of Maggie and the golden bannock:

The River Leader flows past Oxton and meets the Kelphope Burn beside the roundabout at Carfraemill. The Kelphope Burn comes from the valley that leads to Tollishill, which was the setting for a famous Border tale, the story of Midside Maggie and the Duke of Lauderdale.

In the 17th century there were three farms at Tollishill, in upper Lauderdale, under the shadow of Lammer Law. One was tenanted by Robert Hardie, who married Margaret Lylestone of Westruther in 1643. Since the farm was in the middle of the three, Margaret came to be known as "Midside Maggie." The farm was 366 metres (1,200 ft) up and there was a succession of severe and prolonged winters so that there came a time when the young couple found themselves unable to pay the year's rent to the landlord, John, Duke of Lauderdale. Secretly one winter's day Maggie went to tell him so and to plead for time. Lauderdale told Maggie that he would forget all about rent if she could bring him a snowball in June. Deep in a recess of overhanging rock high in the Lammermuirs, Maggie placed a huge hard-packed snowball and daily went to ensure that it remained in good condition within its dark cave. On the last evening of May, Maggie went up in the gloaming to the cave to collect the snowball and take it by horseback over the hill road to Lauder to hammer on the door of Thirlestane Castle in the first June dawn – no doubt to the great surprise of the Duke.

Some years later – in 1650 – Lauderdale was captured at the Battle of Worcester and imprisoned in the Tower of London. Fortune had favoured the couple at Midside and, as they had been prospering, they decided to pay the Duke the rent he had written off. Maggie rode to London with it, a harrowing, hazardous and weary journey.

Thus it came about that one day as John, the now impoverished Duke of Lauderdale, brooded in his room within the Tower, he heard from outside the walls a sweet voice singing the Borders song, *Leader Haughs and Yarrow*. He asked that the singer be brought to see him. "A beggar maid with a bannock for the Duke," announced the servant, ushering in Maggie, and when she and the Duke were alone she broke the big Border bannock and a wealth of gold coins rolled out on to the tablecloth. There was no question of carrying such treasure where it could be seen or the jingle of it heard, through such a place as London. The money helped to pay the ransom for Lauderdale's freedom and he went into exile in Holland. In 1660 he returned to Thirlestane Castle and, remembering, went to Tollishill, where, as a memento of the "golden bannock," he presented Maggie with a silver waist chain or girdle which today can be seen in the National Museum of Antiquities in Edinburgh.

For background information, the Battle of Worcester came about as follows: The English parliament under the influence of the republican-minded Oliver Cromwell, denounced Charles I as a tyrant and had him executed. The Scots, placing their faith in the monarchy and the Covenant crowned his son Charles II at Scone in 1651. They then invaded England in a bid to impose Presbyterianism on the rest of Britain, only to be defeated at the Battle of Worcester by Cromwell's forces.

## The Herring Way

There was a wool trade to the Continent and to reach a seaport from Lauderdale it was more convenient to go over by Lammer Law to Dunbar than it was to take a route to Leith. All these roads were made to avoid the marshy glens of Soutra, before Telford surmounted these problems and made the road we know as the A68. Evidence of this medieval road to Dunbar is still visible as it climbs up from Lauderdale on to the Soutra Plateau and heads in a north-easterly direction. The road at this point is marked on Ordnance Survey maps as a track. This road is usually referred as the Old Fish Road or the Herring Way.

This route would have been busy in autumn, as wool and other merchandise from Lauderdale and beyond were carried to Dunbar.

This coincided with the availability of herrings and small barrels of salted herring would have been carried back on the return jourey

With reference to Thomas Telfer, he designed the bridge at Pathhead carrying the A68 over the Tyne Water. This magnificent bridge is built from stone, 20.7 metres (68 ft) high and has five spans of 14.6 metres (48 ft).

It was completed in 1831 and is a smaller version of the Dean Bridge over the Water of Leith in Edinburgh. Both bridges were completed in the same year.

# Flodden

In 1513, one of the largest Scottish armies marched over Soutra and down through Channelkirk. King James IV of Scotland was never an admirer of his brother-in-law, Henry VIII of England, and observers forecast that their two countries would soon be at war.

In the summer of 1513, Henry, headstrong and ambitious, invaded France, whose Queen appealed to James's well-known sense of chivalry to come to her rescue by invading England. The Queen of

Plate 28: The Master Gunner, Robert Borthwick, fell to his knees and implored the King to let him open fire on the English Army at Flodden. Picture painted by John Mackay

France sent James a sapphire ring as a token of friendship. James wore the ring on his way to Flodden.

Messengers would have come to the village of Channelkirk and the local hamlets, farms and watermills with a list of the number of men of fighting age each establishment had to provide. In the case of tenant farmers, the number of men to be provided was proportional to the amount of acres held in tenancy. The contingent from Channelkirk, along with the other men from the Leader Valley, were allocated a mustering point near Duns. Some days later, all the Borderers joined together and marched south to cross the River Tweed at Coldstream.

Another mustering point was the Bore Stone. At the top of Morningside Road in Edinburgh there is an iron plaque with the inscription:

"The Bore Stone – In which the Royal Standard was last pitched for the muster of the Scottish army on the Borough-muir before the battle of Flodden 1513."

On the plaque is also a quote from Sir Walter Scott's poem *Marmion:*

> Highest and midmost, was descried
> The Royal Banner floating wide;
> The staff, a pine tree strong and straight,
> Pitched deeply in a massive stone,
> Which still in memory is shown,
> Yet bent beneath the standard's weight.

Work on the artillery continued busily until the eve of Flodden, at which there were, according to the Accounts of the Lord High Treasurer, 17 guns altogether, five large cannon, two large culverines, four small culverines and six medium culverines all under the direction of an ancestor of mine, Robert Borthwick.

Robert Borthwick is credited with the casting of the famous cannon "The Seven Sisters" which were guns of great power and beauty. The five large cannon were almost certainly part of the "The Seven Sisters". Robert Borthwick was a skilled gunner and gunsmith, and in charge of artillery at the battle, which might have had a different result had the king taken his advice.

The tale is told of Borthwick falling on his knees before the king, begging permission to fire, and James refusing, declaring he would meet his adversary on equal terms and not with advantage (Plate 28, page 86).

The larger guns were drawn by 36 oxen each and nine drivers. The smaller guns only required eight oxen each. A crane was taken for slinging the guns onto their beds; gun-stones were borne in baskets by 28 horses; and there were at least 12 carts of gun powder. Perhaps in excess of 20,000 men would have passed down through Channelkirk on that day.

In *Marmion*, Sir Walter Scott describes the scene:

> They saw, slow rolling on the plain,
> Full many a baggage cart and wain,
> And dire artillery's clumsy car,
> By sluggish oxen tugged to war;
> And there were Borthwick's Sisters Seven,
> And culverins which France had given.
> Ill-omened gift! The guns remain
> The conqueror's spoil on Flodden plain.

Robert was killed at the start of the encounter by an English cannonball. This happened before the main battle started. William, the Third Lord of Borthwick was also killed in the battle. Nearly every family in Channelkirk Parish lost at least one member on Flodden Field.

Lord Surrey, who commanded the English army, had been allowed by the Prior of Durham to carry the sacred banner of St Cuthbert, which had protected the English in so many previous encounters.

Although the reasons are different, there is a similar incident during Operation Barbarossa. This was the German codename for the invasion of Russia in 1941. The following is a quote from Harrison Salisbury's book, *The Nine Hundred Days:* "With the telephone at General Pavlov's headquarters in Minsk constantly ringing with reports of German attacks, Defence Commissar Timoshenko called from Moscow and ordered Pavlov to take no action against the Germans without prior notification to Moscow. Then he added 'Comrade Stalin has forbidden opening artillery fire against the Germans'." Comrade Stalin was not one to be disobeyed!

My late father, who joined the Royal Artillery at the start of the Second World War, had a good knowledge of ancient artillery pieces, and was sure that he had identified one of the Borthwick's "Sisters Seven" that had been captured at Flodden Field and was now at Woolwich. When he went back after the war, a German bomb had been dropped in the vicinity of the gun and everything was buried in a pile of debris.

Since writing about the Scottish artillery and Robert Borthwick, new information has come to hand. Recently my brother John showed me a letter he received from Colonel Guinan, a friend of my late father, in which there is evidence that Robert Borthwick did not die at Flodden and that all of the "Sisters Seven" were at the battle. I have attached a copy of this letter in Appendix 3 together with information from his booklet *British Artillery before 1859.* I am indebted to Colonel Guinan for permission to use this information.

## Cold war defences

On top of Soutra, about 200 metres east of the most southern of the two sheep tunnels under the road, there is an abandoned Ministry of Defence radiation monitoring station.

On the surface is a small concrete monitoring tower just over one metre high and a sealed entrance to an underground bunker which contains one room. This was manned during the Cold War.

The Cold War was a remorseless struggle for the upper hand by all means short of actual fighting between the Communist and non-Communist powers after the Second World War.

In the mid to late 1980s, Mikhail Gorbachev, the former leader of the Soviet Union, launched his initiatives of Glasnost and Perestroika, which relieved a lot of tension between the Eastern Block nations and the West and effectively ended the Cold War. However, the bunker was only manned by local members of the Royal Observer Corps from 1964 until the mid-1970s. Stow and Lauder had similar monitoring stations.

## Kate's Cauldron

Heading north on the road over Soutra there is the Linn Dean Wildlife Reserve funded by Scottish Natural Heritage using Heritage Lottery money.

The reserve is on the right just before the road starts descending Soutra Hill and is of special interest to the botanist.

In the middle of the reserve is the spectacular valley of the Linn Dean Water and a waterfall which cascades into a deep pool. This place is locally known as Kate's Cauldron.

Plate 29: A snowplough tries to clear blocked road on Soutra in 1957.
Reproduced courtesy of Scotsman Publications Ltd

Care is required, as the ground in the valley is steep and the
footpaths overgrown.

## Soutra snows

There are many tales told of the of the severe winters on Soutra
(Plate 29). At the beginning of January 1979, there was a severe
blizzard and snow drifts up to four-and-a-half metres deep (15 feet)
lay everywhere.

Elspeth's sister and brother-in-law Mary and Kevin from New
Zealand were spending a holiday with us at New Channelkirk.
Kevin came with me to prod for buried sheep. He remarked that the
icy wind and the altitude presented a rarefied atmosphere and he
felt that he was losing touch with reality. He said "no wonder St
Cuthbert had his vision up here". Soon afterwards we found three
layers of Blackface sheep buried in one drift. One sheep was

suffering from hypothermia. We brought it down from the hill by sledge and nursed it back to health.

Later the same winter, another tale was told in *The Southern Reporter* in March 1979.

> **Miraculous escape on Soutra thanks to mystery men**
>
> Bus driver John Fallen and his solitary student passenger escaped death by minutes on snow-wracked Soutra Hill. And this week, in an exclusive interview with *The Southern*, they spoke of their ordeal, and an amazing snatch to safety. For the young student from Dalkeith left the Edinburgh-to-Newcastle bus to get help, and landed up to his shoulders in snowdrifts and a peat bog. Eventually his shouts brought Mr Fallen on to the scene, and a little later they set out for safety. Again their luck was with them, and from out of nowhere two farmers appeared and gave them a lift back to the Carfraemill Hotel. Locals claimed that it was the worst blizzard for several years.

## Dun Law

In 1978 there was a meeting in the Oxton Memorial Hall to debate the use of renewable energy. There were presentations from the South of Scotland Electricity Board, the mining community and the renewable energy lobby. At this time, wind turbines on Dun Law were discussed as a possibility for a community initiative.

In 2000, the construction of 26 wind turbines on Dun Law was completed. Dun Law is situated on the centre of the Soutra Plateau and the wind turbines dominate the Border and the Lothian skyline. The towers are 40 metres high and the three blade turbines are 47 metres in diameter and are capable of producing 660kw for each unit. The turbines are grouped either side of the A68 road.

CHAPTER 5

In Roman times, Dere Street traversed this area. Because of this, the site is of historical interest and it has become the norm for such places to be excavated prior to any building work.

Construction work has started for another 35 windmills in the vicinity of Dun Law. During October and November 2007, a small section of the Dere Street is presently being excavated. Archaeologists found that below the cobbles of the road were birch branches laid parallel with each other. Where the peat was particularly waterlogged, logs were also used.

A repaired section of the road showed that further cobbles had been added. The reason for the excavation was that the road for some of the new windmills had to cross Dere Street and that presented the opportunity for an archaeological dig before the new road was laid.

# Around Oxton and the Railway

## Braefoot

An interesting building in the area is Braefoot (Plate 30, page 96), situated at the junction of the Kirktonhill-Hartside road. A stone bearing the engraving J.B. 1843 witnesses the fact that Braefoot was built by John Borthwick in that year.

Originally the cottage was part of a hamlet of four or five houses. In the 19th Century it accommodated a smith shop, a joiner shop and several families and, at this time, the blacksmith Mr Reid lived there.

The cottage lies at the foot of a brae and in the 19th Century was the venue of a game like shinty. The young men of the village had to roll a leaden cannon-like ball along the ground and down the brae to hit various targets.

In the 20th Century the thatch was removed and the Scots tile roof put on.

Plate 30: Braefoot at the junction of Kirktonhill and Hartside roads

In 1937, Johnny and Isa Weir moved into the cottage. Isa bred dogs, and her spaniels, West Highland terriers and Yorkshire terriers were well known. She even showed at Crufts and sold her dogs as far afield as Moscow. She took in dogs for boarding and hated to put them in the outside kennels. Sometimes between 20 and 30 barking dogs streamed out of the house when Mrs Weir went to answer the doorbell. She also had cats, a goldfish, a parakeet and about 60 canaries in an outside aviary.

Johnny Weir was particularly fond of the parakeet. One day it escaped and Johnny was distraught. He looked high and low for several days, but no sign of the bird. My brother lives in the next valley about 7 km away as the crow flies. By chance, in a telephone conversation, my brother mentioned to me that he had seen a strange bird in a tree. After telling Johnny, he drove across and called the parakeet by name. After a while, the parakeet appeared, flew down and landed on Johnny's shoulder.

Johnny Weir died in 1985 and Elspeth helped Isa Weir to arrange the funeral. Along with other documents in a box under the bed was Johnny's school leaving report. The headmaster of the school near Peebles indicated that Johnny was a bright pupil who could have gone far. Unfortunately he had to leave school at 14 years old to start work. At that time, opportunities for further study would have been extremely limited for people working in the countryside. Today, further and higher education is within the reach of many more people.

The village of Oxton is also known on the high seas. Johnny and Isa's son, David, joined the Royal Navy when he was young. While on board ship, one of his duties was to deliver mail. He was surprised to deliver a letter with an Oxton postmark to one of the ship's officers written by a young lady in the village.

While cruising through the Panama Canal, my wife's cousin from Johannesburg was dining at the captain's table. She asked the captain where he came from. "A small village in the Scottish Borders, which you will not have heard of, called Oxton," replied the captain.

## Airhouse Quarry

After the Second World War, Johnny Weir and Ernie Miller worked at Airhouse Quarry. In the late 1920s, stone from the quarry was used in improving the road over Soutra. Up until this time the road was little more than a grass track. Farms in the area all hired out horses and carts to transport the stone. Buses started running over Soutra in 1928 and this helped to bring about the closure of the passenger service on the railway to Oxton. The road over Soutra was fenced in 1953 and before this time motorists had to beware of Blackface sheep on the road. After the war the equipment at the quarry was modernised and a stone crusher introduced. However, the stone was found to be too soft and commercial quarrying ceased in the 1960s.

The Flynns, who worked the quarry in the 1970s on a much reduced scale, then had a scrapyard in the vicinity of the quarry. In the late 1970s, three men with a lorry were seen cutting up metal in the scrapyard.

While not immediately suspicious, the police were eventually called and pursued the three men over the hill to Middletoun. After a long chase they were apprehended at Crookston. The chase was like something out of one of John Buchan's novels.

At the side of the road near the quarry lived an Irishman called Danny Harkins. He lived in a small wooden hut where there was just enough room for a bed, a chair and a fire in the corner. He used to chat to the school children as they passed, mainly about the weather. On a Saturday night he used to walk to Lauder to partake of some refreshment.

One day in the late 1930s, Bertie Mitchell of Collielaw and Jimmy Hogarth of Hartside had been hunting. The story has it that they had stopped in Lauder for some refreshment. At Blackburn, Jimmy got off his horse for nature's call, but when he tried to get on again he could not manage.

Bertie then got off his horse to help Jimmy on to his one, only to find that he could not get on his own horse. This caused Jimmy to get off his horse to help. It ended up with both men having to walk home. This scene was witnessed by a small band of onlookers.

# Tattie fields

When the potato price was high from 1976 to 1981, there were a lot of potatoes grown in the Oxton area. The centre of the operation was Midburn Farm and Tom Rowe, the farmer, rented ground from neighbouring farmers. This provided fresh ground for growing potatoes.

The "tattie picking" necessitated gangs of itinerant workers. Irish brogues were heard in the Tower Hotel, there were extra children in Channelkirk School and extra customers in George Bell's, the grocer.

At a farm south of Oxton, in the 1940s, there was a farmer who was known for his quick temper. One frosty morning in winter his tractor would not start, so he went into his house and returned with his gun and shot the tractor. The tractor's radiator was badly damaged. When I told this story to a friend, she said: "Did the tractor learn its lesson?"

In *The Southern Reporter* in August 1980 there was news of an Oxton farming family.

> **Former Oxton man appearing at Festival**
>
> Born in Haddington and raised in Oxton, 44-year-old Billy Purves is perhaps the only blind actor currently working on the British stage. Billy, blind since he was 19, is appearing in this year's Edinburgh Festival with the Ajjit Theatre Company, and plays a cottar in their acclaimed *Folk and the Land* production. He left Haddington at the age of seven when his father Andrew, a joiner in the town, decided to move during the war and became a tenant farmer at Bowerhouse, near Oxton.

In the mid-1950s Andrew Purves grew potatoes for Hogg the potato merchant in Dalkeith. The potatoes were harvested by a

Plate 31: Old Inchkeith Steading

tractor pulling a spinner. The blades of the spinner bring the potatoes to the surface so that they can be hand picked by the potato squad.

Andy Hume told me the following story: One October the squad of tattie pickers from Dalkeith arrived at Bowerhouse. These women were locally known as "Hoggy's Angels". The tattie pickers complained that Andrew Purves was driving the tractor too fast and when he did not slow down, they went on strike and started pelting him with tatties. He had to retreat into the farmhouse. Later, when he ventured out of the house, he discovered that the tattie pickers had gone home to Dalkeith. They refused to come back again to Bowerhouse. This left Andrew with a problem. How are the tatties going to be lifted?

On most farms the potatoes were picked by school children, who got two weeks holiday from school in October to pick them. This was generally referred to as the tattie picking holiday. Andrew got in touch with the Education Department and the school children in Oxton, who went to secondary school in Duns and Earlston, were given an extra weeks holiday to pick the tatties at Bowerhouse.

## Inchkeith Farm

On travelling through Bowerhouse and proceeding southwest, Inchkeith Farm is reached. About 1 km away from Inchkeith, and positioned on the route of the Girthgate, are the ruins of an old steading. This is old Inchkeith originally one of the Lauderdale Estate farms (Plate 31). In 1950 it was bought by Bonnyrigg shopkeepers John and Janet Wilkinson and then farmed by their late son, Derek, and now by their grandson.

The steading was abandoned in the early 1960s and a new steading built on a more advantageous site.

There is a story told that John Wilkinson kept a Blue-grey cow to supply milk to the families on the farm. The cow had the free range of the farm. John was planting potatoes by hand in the steep field beside the old steading and, at a distance behind him, the cow was picking them up and eating them. I have a copy of the sale document drawn up by the Lauderdale Estates and it differs from the steadings of today. It included byres for cows, stabling for horses, calf pen, turnip house, pig house and hen house.

There is a story concerning a three-year-old boy. In the late afternoon, on a foggy day in December 1953, the boy disappeared from Hartside. His grandfather was the shepherd on the farm. About 30 or 40 people turned up to look for the boy, and searched with torches until about 2am, but no sign of him could be found. The next morning, Jimmy Laing, the shepherd at the Den, found him lying, fast asleep, in the heather on top of Soutra. The boy must have travelled about three miles.

## Brae Cottage

John Mackay, a noted historian and illustrator, lived in Brae Cottage in Oxton with his wife, Kay. During the war, Kay was John's driver and she continued to drive him around. He never learnt to drive. John died in 1999, his wife having died some years earlier. Brae Cottage lies downhill from the Tower Hotel in a road which has no name plate. Most villagers refer to it as The Brae or even think of it as an extension of The Loan (see page 108), but on the latest council plans it is marked as Cemetery Road.

John's father had Mackays Toffee Doddle shop in Fountainbridge in Edinburgh. John was born in 1910 in the same stair in Fountainbridge as Sean Connery. There is a story told about Sir Sean. After leaving school, he worked on a milk round for the Co-operative Society. When he mentioned to his boss that he was going to leave and take up acting, his boss advised him against it and said: "In four or five years you could have a horse and cart." In those days, the Co-op delivered the milk using horses and carts.

John wrote and illustrated a number of books, as well as being a contributor to *The Scots Magazine* and other publications. His watercolour paintings, mainly of local scenes, were well known and two of them appear in this book. My wife was at school at Umtali in Zimbabwe in the 1940s and 1950s and when we came to live here, she was fascinated to discover that the history book she had at school had been illustrated by John.

## Ploughmen make their mark

The *Southern Reporter* of October 1974 records that two Lauderdale ploughmen took top honours at the British National Championship Ploughing Match. Bob Anderson, Nether Howden and John

Gilchrist, Threeburnford, Oxton, travelled to Fawley Court in Hereford to challenge 127 ploughmen from all over the British Isles. Bob, reigning Scottish champion, was representing Scotland and John was ploughing for his local association.

Both competed in the semi-digger class where John came first and Bob third. Then they went on to compete in the plough-off where Bob took the reserve championship. He was only seven points behind the winner and his performance earned him the chance to travel to Canada the following September to compete in the world championships. John was seventh equal in the final.

The two Borderers had to plough half an acre of stubble in two-and-threequarter hours. Bob used a Ford 400 tractor and a Kvernelands plough while John used a Ford 300 and a Ransoms plough. No stranger to top class ploughing matches, Bob won the British title in 1966 and competed in the world finals in Rhodesia, where he came fifth.

## Lauder Light Railway

My great great-uncle, John Borthwick, lived at Crookston and I have a copy of his submission objecting to the building of the railway in 1897. I also have a copy of the *Order of the Light Railway Commissioners* "Authorizing the Construction of a Light Railway between Fountainhall Railway Station and Lauder in the Counties of Midlothian and Berwick".

The Lauder Light Railway was 17 km (10.5 miles) long and single track throughout except for a passing place at Oxton. The railway gauge was 4ft 8in which is the standard British gauge. The original Edinburgh and Dalkeith Railway gauge was 4ft 6in. Isambard Kingdom Brunel, the famous 19th Century engineer constructed the Great Western Railway from London to Bristol with a 7ft gauge.

The route was closed to passenger traffic in September 1932. Thereafter the railway carried freight only and was closed to all

Plate 32: Railway Station, Oxton after 1910. The driver is standing on the train's footplate. © The Trustees of the National Museums of Scotland

traffic in September 1958. In the early 1950s the last goods train passed through Oxton (Plate 32). There is still a sign at the side of the road entering Oxton where the station was situated that says:

> LONDON & NORTH EASTERN RAILWAY
>
> WARNING TO TRESPASSERS
>
> The London & North Eastern Railway Company hereby give warning to all persons not to trespass upon any of the Railways, Stations, Works, Lands or Property belonging to or worked by the Company.
>
> Trespassers are liable to a fine or imprisonment for every offence.
>
> BY ORDER

Now to quote an amusing excerpt from John Mackay's article on the story of the Lauder Light Railway published in *The Scots Magazine* of October 1970:

> There are many pawky stories heard around Oxton regarding the speed of the train and the understanding between driver

and passengers. The folk at Hartside, it is said, would arrange that the train should slow down as it approached the brae up to their farm and they would then cast their parcels and themselves on to a convenient spot by the line. Again, along the route there might be business with milk cans in which both driver and guard would co-operate. "Have I time, do you think," a passenger would ask either official "to get out and pick some flowers?" "Ay, but there's nae flooers here," was the answer. "Oh, but I've got a packet of seeds in my pocket," would be the rejoinder.

The speed of the train was curtailed to 40 kmph (25 mph) and to 16 kmph (10 mph) on the curves. The Maggie Lauder railway from Fountainhall to Lauder via Oxton would probably have been a lot safer to travel on than some of our modern trains.

The railway is a great source of local tales. Josh Bennet, when he was young, used to have his hair cut by his father. He always fidgeted too much, so his father used to cut Josh's hair while he was watching the train coming in.

On a foggy day, about two years before the railway closed, a train coming from Lauder hit the late George Bell's bakers van with George in it, and carried it along the line past the Oxton station master's house. George was not hurt. He had just left the shop and the warmth of the freshly baked bread had contributed to steamed-up windows and George not seeing the train coming.

In another incident the train hit the farm egg collection van at Shielfield between Oxton and Lauder. Apparently it was quite a big smash, but the driver was not hurt. One local person said that the back of the van resembled a large omelette.

To forestall a food shortage during the last war, three large sheds were constructed at Lauder station. These sheds mainly stored cereals.

The late Ernie Miller still had a ticket from Eskbank to Oxton.

In the early years of the railway, the goods side flourished. The late Mr James Gilchrist remembers as a boy at the farmhouse of Justicehall being roused in the small dark hours by the barking of the sheepdogs, and then going across to Oxton Station to help, by the light of stable lanterns, with the herding of the flocks into railway wagons. "Oxton is not the busy place it once was," Mr Gilchrist said. "I've seen as many as 33 wagons lined up to take stock away."

There was a newspaper article recently reporting that a local person had seen a ghost train passing through Oxton station.

As a boy, I was brought up at Crookston in the Gala Water valley north of Fountainhall. There were many occasions when the car stopped on the A7 and my brother and I watched excitedly as the train to Oxton crossed the road. The train usually consisted of a small number of goods wagons with a guard's van at the end. The train stopped and the guard walked up the length of the train and closed the gates across the road. The train then crossed the road and the guard opened the gates again, got back on the guard's van and the train disappeared round the bend on the track. In cold weather the guard had a fire burning inside the guard's van and smoke could be seen rising from the chimney.

*The Scotsman* records the impact of snow on the railway in 1915.

*Friday, 19 March 1915*

**Lauder Railway Blocked**

The most severe snowstorm which has been experienced in the Stow and Lauder districts for the last eight years set in early yesterday morning. The fall of snow was exceptionally heavy, and a gale from the north caused serious drifting. The first train from Lauder stuck in the drift about three-quarters of a mile from Oxton, and there remained all day. Attempts were made at handcasting, but the snow was blowing in so rapidly that ultimately the surfacemen gave the work up. Other workmen on the section between Oxton and Fountainhall had the same experience. The line is now more or less blocked throughout.

The Lauder and Oxton mails and newspapers were sent round by Earlston, where they arrived early in the afternoon, but the latter got no further than Lauder, as a man on horseback, who tried to make the journey to Oxton, found this road also impassable – a most unusual occurrence. Traders' carts generally had to give up their rounds, and none of the rural postmen was able to complete the journey. Even on the low ground there was a fall of about ten inches, but reports of wreaths of four or five feet deep on the upland roads are common. In the afternoon the fall ceased and the sun shone for a time, but the wind continued.

Another story from *The Scotsman* is about what might have been and is edited due to its length and detail.

Monday 22 March 1897.

### The Dalkeith and Lauder Light Railway Scheme

In connection with the proposed formation of a light railway from Dalkeith south by Pathhead to Lauder, a deputation visited Lauder on Saturday for the purpose of ascertaining the feeling of parties in that district.

The representatives were members of the committee chosen

at the public meeting held at Dalkeith ten days ago and included Provost Liddell. Driving by Pathhead, Blackshiels, Soutrahill, and Oxton, the party were able to indicate a probable route for the line from Dalkeith, which if proceeded with would be of about twenty miles in length.

A large number of gentlemen of the Lauder district of Berwickshire received the Dalkeith deputation, the joint meeting being held in the Black Bull Hotel, Lauder. Provost Liddell explained the origination of the scheme, and mentioned that north of Soutra there was a very general feeling in favour of the construction of the line from Dalkeith, the district being rich in minerals and also an important agricultural country.

At the end of the meeting, Provost Liddell said that when the deputation came again from Dalkeith in the course of a month or two they might be able to indicate more definitely the outcome of their consideration of the scheme.

Further railway information is given in Appendix 2.

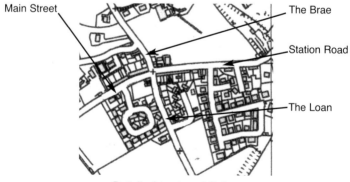

Detail of centre of Oxton

# The Village of Oxton

## Viking roots

The name of Oxton is derived from Ugston, possibly meaning Town of Ulfkill. Ulfkill was probably a Viking name. There is another Oxton near York and one near Nottingham. Perhaps there are others. This has led to mix-ups in postal deliveries and telephone calls.

Today, our village of Oxton is less of a farming community than it used to be and more of the population now commute for their trades and professions. The upper reaches of the Leader Water flows past the village (Plate 33 & Plate 34, pages 110 and 111, show the village in former times).

In Oxton there is still evidence of the past. There are rings to tie up horses on some of the houses in Station Road (page 108). At the rear of the houses on the south side of Station Road runs a much older cobbled "Row", once the main thoroughfare, which is only wide enough to permit the passage of horses and small carts (Plate 35).

A well has been uncovered in The Row near the old town hall. Perhaps this was a water supply for the village.

Every Tuesday afternoon there is a doctor's surgery in a house in The Row. Dr John Crombie Smith is the present doctor, but the house was purchased by his father, Dr Harry Crombie Smith.

Outside the old Smithy in the village there is still a ring for forming cartwheel rims.

## Village school

In Main Street (page 108), uphill from the Tower Hotel, stands a house called Clorabank. (house with the porch in Plate 1, Chapter 1). This is the old Channelkirk School. In 1795 the school was shifted

Plate 33: Main Street, Oxton 1931. Reproduced courtesy of RCAHMS (RS Henderson)

Plate 34 (above): The Main Street, Oxton, in the 1880s showing the Tower Hotel as a thatched cottage

Plate 35 (left): View of the upper part of The Row, Oxton

Plate 36 (left): Jock and Dod Campbell outside Oxton Castle with unknown lady, early 1920s

Plate 37 (below): John Brown from Oxton Mains with a pair of horse outside the Smiddy in Main Street, Oxton, early 1940s. The burnt-out shell of Oxton Castle can be seen in the background

Both photos reproduced courtesy of Flora Pretswell

down hill from Channelkirk to Oxton village. It was found that the children had difficulty reaching Channelkirk in winter. The school and the schoolhouse were one building, the school in the basement and the schoolhouse in the upper storey.

The school was known as "Nicol Dodd's School". The church school was held where the Post Office was in the Loan.

The present Channelkirk School was built in 1865 and in 1866 Henry Marshall Liddell came as headmaster. The school as it is today is the result of a complete refurbishment in 1991/1992.

For a period after the First World War, Clorabank was the Oxton Police Station.

## Oxton Castle

At the top of Main Street is Campbells Yard. At the top of this yard there used to stand a two-storey house called Oxton Castle. It had stairs going up from the road to the first storey.

The last residents included Jock and Dod Campbell who founded Campbells of Oxton (Plate 36). Also downstairs lived Davy Purves, who kept a few cows and grazed them on the roadsides. Davy Purves also had a few ducks who made their home on the Clora Burn.

The house burnt down on New Year's Day 1928. All the residents escaped unharmed (Plate 37).

Campbells of Oxton is still a thriving livestock haulage business today and has a fleet of ten lorries.

Jock and Dod Campbell had a nephew called Jock Campbell.

In the late 1940s the young lads of Oxton used to play football at the cross (crossroads). The second house down The Row from the cross regularly had its pantry window broken. Jock Campbell used to replace the glass, as it was usually his son "Wee Jock" who had broken it. Apparently Jock had a stock of glass to fit most windows near the cross.

In 1978, when Willie Nisbet managed Campbells of Oxton, the local farmers presented him with a return ticket to see the World Cup Football finals in Argentina.

There was no doubt among the fans that Scotland was going to win the World Cup, however, that was not to be. Ally McLeod, the Scotland manager, talked up the chances of winning and the song below epitomizes the starry-eyed view of the fans:

### Ally's Tartan Army

We're on the march wi' Ally's Army,
We're going tae the Argentine,
And we'll really shake them up,
When we win the World Cup,
Cos Scotland is the greatest football team.

Willie Nisbet was also a Heart of Midlothian Football Club fan and in 1998, when Willie was in ill health, Jim Jefferies, the Hearts Manager came to his house to let Willie hold the Scottish Cup. Jim then went to see Robert Young, another Hearts fan in the village, who was in a wheelchair, and let him hold the cup. After this a large crowd gathered in the Tower Hotel to touch the cup and have their photographs taken with it.

## Tower Hotel

The Tower Hotel is still one of the social centres of the community, where stories are swapped and friendships made. The pub is particularly full when Hearts football games are sometimes shown on non-terrestrial TV channels.

In *The Sunday Post* of 31 December 1969, there was a report on Oxton's own football star.

### Stop the game – It's milking time

For my man of '67, I decided to search football's highways and byways and I finally came up with – Billy Gilchrist of Oxton, centre half of Border Amateur League club, Lauder. 25-year-old Billy works on his father's farm and it certainly complicates his football career. Consider last Saturday. He turned out for Lauder against Duns and at exactly 3.20pm the team coach Alec McDonald signalled to Gilchrist to come off. A few yards from the pitch a car was waiting to take Billy straight back to the farm – because at 3.30pm he was due to start milking the cows. It could hardly happen at Ibrox or Celtic Park or Tynecastle.

Alec McDonald coached Lauder AFC to be South of Scotland Amateur Cup Winners in 1969-1970.

In the early 1960s, Dod Gilchrist was more fortunate. He lived in the village and played football on Saturdays. His wife, Doreen, went round to Justicehall with the two children in the pram, and did the milking for him.

# Justicehall

Justicehall, situated on the edge of the village (Plate 38, next page), was built for James Justice of the Court of Session in Edinburgh in the 18th Century. His passion for gardening led him to send to Holland for a cargo of soil to encourage his tulips. His son, Captain James Justice who succeeded to the estate, was less interested in gardens, preferring

Plate 38: Oxton War Memorial Hall on the left with Justicehall in the background

Plate 39: Jim and Elsie Gilchrist at their Diamond Wedding in March 1989

the company of strolling players calling at Justicehall for impromptu concerts at all times of the day and night. This bohemian existence persuaded his wife to leave Justicehall and the Captain. He in time sold the mansion to live modestly in the village.

For a long time the Gilchrists lived at Justicehall. Mr James Gilchrist (Plate 39) became a well known sheepdog handler and breeder and performed , with his dogs Merc and Spot, at the Edinburgh Military Tattoo. James used to take the sheep and his two dogs every night to the Tattoo in his pick-up. The police used to wave him past on his way to the Castle Esplanade, but what they did not realise was that the pick-up was unlicensed.

## Trade and commerce

In 1968 there were still a number of shops and public buildings in Oxton these were:

Mary Scott's sweetie shop, which was particularly popular with school children. On Saturday mornings, there was always a queue of children waiting to sample Mary's freshly made ice cream. Although generations of children remembered it as a sweetie shop, it sold everything from boot laces to hanks of wool, black lead, Brasso and soap. Mary had to explain to the children about war-time rationing and why they could only get 4oz of sweeties a week.

Spence's grocers shop near the bottom of The Row. The Cockburns built the shop in 1904 from which they operated as a trading business. James Spence took over the shop in 1938 and married his wife Davina shortly after.

James Spence had been a fur trader for 11 years with the Hudson Bay Company in Canada before returning to Scotland. Mrs Spence's family had worked at Hutton Castle for William Burrell the

Plate 40: Cockburn's Shop in Station Road, Oxton. Photograph possibly taken in early 1930s. Photographer unknown

shipping magnate. Mr Burrell acquired a wide variety of works of art, which are now housed in the Burrell Collection in Glasgow and Berwick on Tweed. Beside the shop, there was a paraffin store in a shed. Most people would have heated their houses with paraffin heaters. The shop closed about 1975.

A photograph of Cockburn's shop is shown (Plate 40). The ring to tie horses can be seen on the side of the shop and, in the top right of the picture, is a loft door. The horse would have been tied to the ring while the cart would have been loaded with sacks of meal and flour coming down the chute from the loft.

## Postal services

Alec McDonald had the Post Office up the hill in The Loan (page 108). Alec was a former Hibs player. Andy Gilchrist recalls that,

## CHAPTER 7

between the two world wars, there was a postman called Alec Sandilands who only had one arm. He had an artificial limb with a hook at the end. He set out on his postal rounds at 6.30am to deliver the mail to the village and the outbye farms. After delivering post to the village, his round included Airhouse, New Channelkirk, Carfrae, Hillhouse, Tollishill, Fairnylees, Headshaw, Glengelt and Kirktonhill. He would cover at least 17 miles on foot in an average day and arrive back in the village about 3pm. He only delivered mail to some of the outlying cottages, such as Friar's Nose, twice a week.

In the Post Office there was a postmistress of varying temperament, described by one villager as just "plain crabbit". She liked an orderly queue in the Post Office and on the pavement outside and not too much hilarity. Alec Sandilands used to get a row from her if he was five minutes early or five minutes late.

If the winter was severe, some farmers and shepherds used to meet Alec at a pre-arranged time and place to receive their mail. When Alec retired, Bill Fullerton took over and used a bicycle to assist him with the postal round. The late Ian Sutherland tells the story of a previous postman on the same round who was a retired shepherd. One farmer did not have time to bury a sheep before the postman arrived, and not wishing the postman to notice it, he propped it up until the postman had passed.

Just before Christmas, Elspeth and I had parked our car in Lauder when a post van drove up and blocked us in. The postie came up to Elspeth and asked if we were going to be doing some shopping or should he move his van. Elspeth said not to worry as she had things to do, to which he replied: "Thank goodness because I have to wait for my computer to tell me when I can empty the post box. You see even if I am one minute early I will get a phone call

Plate 41 (above): Beverley Dorward and Jim Harris outside the Bakehouse Store, Oxton. Reproduced courtesy of William Brodie

Plate 42 (left): George Bell with his grocer's van on his last round before retirement

tomorrow from Head Office in Edinburgh ticking me off because it all gets recorded and relayed to their computer. If I am ten minutes late, they will want to know where I have been!" The postie showed us his computer which looked like a large mobile phone.

Alec Sandilands had a son called Eddie who joined the merchant navy and became a radio officer. In about 1950 he emigrated to Australia and got a job with OTC, the communications company. Eddie was sent on an expedition to Antarctica as radio officer. During this time he climbed one of the mountains which is now marked on the map of Antarctica as Mount Sandilands.

## Bread and rolls

There was Bells the bakers shop, where Jim Fullerton used to bake bread. Many people can remember buying warm bread and rolls freshly baked. The children used to wait for the school bus in the warm bakehouse and dry their coats from the heat of the warm ovens on a wet day. The bakehouse closed in the early 1960s. Liz Maddock ran the shop for a while and now Beverley Dorward and Jim Harris run this shop as a general store and sub Post Office (Plate 41). The shop has recently been expanded and opening hours extended.

Recently, while in Jenners store in Edinburgh, Elspeth and I were talking to a member of the sales staff who told us that her husband's grandfather was the baker in Oxton. His name was Preston and he had 12 or 13 children. The old baking oven is still visible in the shop.

George Bell used to leave his shop early in the morning with his van to take groceries to families in the outlying districts. Many people, particularly the frail and elderly, depended on George for their provisions. About 1990 George had to give up his grocery round due to poor health (Plate 42).

Plate 43: View looking up from the bottom of The Row. The old village hall is the two-storey building on the left

It is the only shop left in the village. Oxton still had a police station and Alec Denholm was the policeman. Also there is the village hall called the Oxton War Memorial Hall in Station Road (Plate 38, page 116) which was built in 1924 to replace the old village hall in the Row (Plate 43).

## Annfield Inn

There were two shops before 1968 that deserve a mention, the first is Annfield Inn (Plate 5, Chapter 1). Annfield Inn was a solitary licensed house situated half-way between Glengelt and Carfraemill on the A68 road. The inn was opened in 1832.

Latterly, Laura Graham ran a shop which sold soft drinks and confectionary. Many people remember her for the dangly earrings and broad-brimmed hat which she wore.

Mrs Graham had no scales to weigh the sweets so she used to walk, almost 2 km (1.5 miles) to Oxton to get the sweets weighed in Mary Scott's shop.

The building was knocked down in the road widening programme in the late 1950s/early 1960s. There is a rowan tree close to the spot where Annfield Inn used to stand. The remains of the water supply for Annfield Inn can be seen just over 0.4 km (0.25 mile) north of the Oxton turn-off in the field on the west side of the road.

Mrs Graham then went to live with her son, Gibbie, in the middle cottage at Kirktonhill.

About 1980, my wife and I went to visit Mrs Graham, who was now in her 90s and, during the conversation, she said "the laddie will put on the tea", Gibbie being 74 at that time. Gibbie was the local roadman before Ernie Miller, although for most of his life he had been a mole and rabbit catcher as, indeed, was his father, William Graham.

At Heathfield, on the corner of the Oxton crossroads, a lintel above the door reads "Ironmonger and Seedsman". This was Mr Matthewson's shop. He also was the postmaster and ran the Post Office in the Loan (Plate 44, page 124).

His gravestone is beside the church bell rope in Channelkirk graveyard, and reads:

"Roualeyn Wm Matthewson merchant and village post master for over half a century died Feb 1930 aged 75 years". A 90-year-old cousin of his visited the village recently.

Plate 44 (above): View from The Loan, Oxton, circa 1938. Business names in view include The Tower Hotel; J M Matthewson, stationer & newsagent. Reproduced courtesy of the University of St Andrews Library

Plate 45 (left): Tossing the Caber at Oxton Games, August 1936. R Harkness tossing the cable, and the judge making notes. Scottish Borders Council, Museum and Gallery Service Collection

# Oxton Reel

In Book 6 of *The Scottish Country Dance Book* is printed the music
and instructions for the Oxton Reel. The reel is from Bremner's
Collection of 1757 and was danced in the village in 1932.

In 1983 the Oxton Reel was again danced in the War Memorial
Hall by local people. The dance is done in Strathspey time, is very
graceful and was performed at several different venues to support
local festivities and charities. The dance was then performed to
celebrate the Queen's Golden Jubilee in 2002.

# Oxton Games

Oxton used to hold a professional games. This took place annually
in June or July and included running events and heavy events such
as tossing the caber (Plate 45), throwing the sheaf over the bar, and
tug-of-war between local teams.

The tug-of-war between Oxton and Lauder being particularly
closely contested with neither side willing to give ground. The late
Ian Brady was enthusiastically involved in the organisation of the
games.

Various well-known characters were seen at the games including
Goeff Capes, the strongest British man at that time; and George
McNeil, the sprinter from Musselburgh who broke several Scottish
records.

One year my wife, Elspeth, and young son, Malcolm, were sitting
on a bench and a gentleman sat down beside them and offered
Malcolm a sweet.

This gentleman was Mick McGahey, the vice-president of the
National Union of Mine Workers. Support for the games dwindled
and they were discontinued in the mid-1990s.

In *The Southern Reporter* in January 1979 the following article appeared:

### Bright future ahead for Oxton youngster

Fifteen-year-old David Douglas of Oxton has every reason to look pleased with himself. On Saturday he won the 1,600 metres title and the Jimmy Gibson Memorial Trophy at Meadowbank in great style, putting in a blistering last lap to leave his opponents trailing in his wake.

Trained by Selkirk's Jack Knox and Keith Carver of Galashiels, David has spent the last two months preparing for the race.

The blizzards at the beginning of January made it impossible for him to reach Selkirk for training, so instead his father – former half-miler Bill Douglas – kept him hard at work in the snowy wastes around Oxton.

David had been involved in track running since the age of ten, and there seemed little doubt that this Border youngster has a bright future ahead on the professional games circuit.

After leaving school, David continued with his running and served a joinery apprenticeship with Billy Nisbet. He now lives in America with his Irish wife.

## Oxton Quoiting Challenge

About two years ago , Dave Waldie ploughed up a quoit near the Oxton road end. This is where the game of quoits used to be played in Oxton and competitors from Oxton and surrounding areas competed for the Oxton Quoiting Challenge Cup. The first winner was in 1902 and the last winner was T Bell, George Bell's Uncle, in 1933.

Each competitor was given two quoits to throw and they had to
land over a hen's feather sticking out of the ground. The ground
round the hen's feather was puddled clay and the quoit did not
move much after landing. Quoiting dates back to the Pentathlon of
ancient Greece.

The quoiting cup is now one of the flower show cups and still
bears the names of the quoiting winners. An extract from the
Flower Show Committee meeting of January 1974 reads as follows:

> The Secretary then intimated he had a conversation with Mr
> C Brown, Rigside asking if the Horticultural Society would
> be interested in taking possession of the Championship Cup
> belonging to the Quoiting Club. The meeting discussed the
> suggestion and decided to accept with the following ideas to
> clean and polish, yet another base, and insure it and return it
> to the Quoiting Club when requested. It was suggested that
> it should be awarded for the best tomatoes in the show.

There were many activities and societies which flourished in
Oxton and in *Rutherfurd's Southern Counties' Register and
Directory,* published in 1866, the following two societies are
recorded:

> Oxton Bovial Society – Instituted 1835 for the purpose of
> helping working men, such as hinds and shepherds, in the
> event of their cow dying, to get another. Each member, on an
> average, pays 4s. per annum; and if his cow dies he is
> allowed £8 to help to get another.
> Total Abstinence Society (instituted 1840). Business is
> conducted by a committee of eight members, who meet twice
> a year. The Society has an annual soiree in January and a
> rural excursion and picnic in July.

Also among the list of trades in Oxton appears "Matthewson, James, grocer, seedsman, and ironmonger" and "Reid, James & Alexander, blacksmiths."

The minute books of the Oxton Bovial Society are held by the Scottish Borders Council Archives, now in Hawick. The Bovial Society wound up its affairs in 2002 and money from the society provided wooden gates for the Channelkirk church car park.

## Far and wide

In the mid-1980s our friends, Dudley and Beth Warner and their son, Charles, from Nashville, Tennessee, came to stay with us. Dudley is a property developer and, on his return, named his next development in Nashville, Oxton Hill. Two of the roads are called Oxton Hill Lane and Channelkirk Lane. Shortly after his visit, he phoned up from Nashville to say that he had heard on the news that Soutra had been blocked by snow.

About 59 new houses have been built in Oxton, the two main housing developments being Justice Park and St Cuthbert's View. To cope with this increase in population, the village now has an additional water supply and a sewage treatment works.

## Community life

In 2005 there was discussion about whether the Channelkirk Primary School in Oxton should be closed and the pupils sent to a new school to be built five miles away in Lauder.

A headline in *The Border Telegraph* on 30 August, 2005 read:

**School closure "ghost town" fears**

Members of the Scottish Borders Council's education executive will decide next week if Channelkirk, which has a

roll of 54 primary and 11 nursery pupils, is to undergo a
statutory consultation on closure.

In December 2005, the Council voted not to close the school on
the recommendation of the Director of Education who, the Council's
own website reported, said: "The strength of the community feeling,
the school's size (54 pupils) and the sustainable nature of the school
roll, together with the environmental impact of transporting so
many children, has in this instance persuaded me that closure
should not be pursued."

I hope that this little book will inspire other people to take notes
of their area. It has been my privilege to do this and has been such a
pleasure.

# Epilogue

This talk has touched on the history of the area including the Romans and St Cuthbert, the history of the church, some ministers and their times, Channelkirk graveyard, Upper Lauderdale and the Soutra Plateau, the area around Oxton and the railway, and the village of Oxton.

The past, present and the future are all part of the same thing, and this moment will already be the past and be history by the time we leave the hall.

Thank you,


H.B.
Channelkirk Cottage
November 2007

# Appendix 1 – Lammermoor Leaves

The note and the three poems which follow are from a collection called *Lammermoor Leaves* by A.T.G. and published by the *Border Advertiser* in 1898.

Some personal observations about the three poems:

First poem: *Old Airhouse Wood*
The position of Airhouse is across the narrow valley from Channelkirk Church. There is still an ancient wood on the slopes below Airhouse Farm.

Second poem: *A Lammermoor Legend*
This legend ties up with the story on page 70

Third poem: *The Minister Militant*
Thomas Brown would probably have been the John Brown referred to on page 44. This could tie in with the date the poem was written and the title *The Minister Militant*.
John Brown's wife was Philis Moscrop, not Betty.
Millmount would be Mountmill referred to on page 43
The two stout Hibernians would have been Irishmen.
The glebe was the church land to the west of the church.
The Holy Well is referred to on page 28.
Most of the other names in the poem still exist, but the order in which they appear in the poem make no sense.

NOTE: This little book is a Collection of "Leaves" gathered for the most part on the lower slopes of the "Lammermoor" Hills during Autumn holidays. In the folds of the *Berwickshire News*, the *Border Advertiser*, or the *Border Magazine,* they have been already pressed.

They are here stitched together for the sake of those who desire to preserve for a few days longer some simple thoughts they were pleased to value. These "Leaves" shall fade, as all leaves do. Till then, they may bear a memory of "The waters trinklin' doun amang the fern."

# Old Airhouse Wood

Around Old Airhouse Wood
  There breaks the morning sheen,
The golden light appears
  Above the Kirktown dean.

Here Cuthbert roamed of yore
  With shepherd plaid and rod,
And here in heav'nly dream
  He tarried with his God.

Above Old Airhouse Wood
  Full noon its blaze doth shed;
The holy waters clear
  Seek Leader's pebbly bed.

And Channelkirk stands fair,
  To Cuthbert's mem'ry reared;
And grassy mounds are seen,
  With grave-stones wond'rous weird.

Along Old Airhouse Wood
The length'ning shadows fall
And day's bright beams have sped
From saintly Cuthbert's hall.

Yet hallow'd is the scene,
 And mystic thoughts crowd fast,
As, wand'ring through the wood,
We muse, and mourn the past.

Farewell! Old Airhouse Wood;
 Thy mantle green inspires
To link the passing hour
  With mem'ries of our sires.

Saint Cuthbert! Thou thy work
  Did'st well and fearlessly:
We follow in thy steps,
And holy visions see.

Where mountain streamlets three
  In Leader's source all meet,
Of old there lived a man
  Whose story here repeat.

# A Lammermoor Legend

He led a frugal life,
  His barn was filled with store;
His wife had simple ways,
  As women had of yore.

John was a willful man,
  And spake ofttimes with ire,
Nor did his wife allow
  To frustrate his desire.

Many a year had gone
  Since they did each repair
At sound of Sabbath bell
  To God's own House of Prayer.

And yet "for sake o' look"
They rested all that day;
With conscience in a sleep,
  They wiled the hours away.

In early days of May
  The waters ran in flood,
The wind did howl and rage
  As if in angry mood.

The farmer rose one morn
  To view Field Pikiestone,
And vowed to sow his pease
  Whene'er the floods had gone.

At length the storm did cease,
  The sun shone out on high;
The farmer joyed to see
  Field Pikiestone quite dry.

To's wife the farmer said,
  "The morrow morn will see
"My eident hand at work
 "A-sawin' I shall be."

Na, na, guidman, na,na,
  "I'll daur ye that tae dae;
"The Sawbath o' the Lord!
  "Ye'll rest, and read, and pray.

"My faither an' his fore
  "Aye keept the Sawbath day;
"Ye'll never hope tae thrive
  "Gin ye aince disobey."

Thus Jean did say. But John
  Was  stubborn as a mule.
"Gae wa', ye bleth'rin tyke,"
  He spoke as doth the fool.

"I care na for your fouk,
  "Ye're eedyats ane an' a'
"The morn's the Sawbath day!
  "My crap o' pease I'll saw."

To couch, but not to sleep,
  Did John and Jean repair;
And oft the good dame said
  "Beware, guidman, beware."

The morning sun shone bright,
  Above the Meikle Law,
And John rose up at dawn
  "My crap o' pease I'll saw."

Jean spake once more.  Her eyes
Were flooded full with tears;
"Guidman, bide in the hoose,
  "Your wife the Lord's voice hears.

"He speaks richt doun frae he'ven,
  "He rides upon the cl'ud,
"He sends the lichtnin' forth,
  "He roars in thunder l'ud."

John was a willful man;
  His wife he heeded not;
He's gone to Pikiestone
  The day was clear and hot.

He sowed his pease, and thought
  As rose the mid-day sun,
How happy was his lot!
  His sowing all but done!

But, hark! A distant sound!
  The gath'ring cloud appears;
The lightnings vivid flash!
  The thunder loud he hears.

Jean takes the Holy Book
  (It bore the dust of years),
She scarce could read the page
  Through all the mist of tears.

A louder, nearer crash!
  The rattling of the pane!
The fiery fork and ball!
  The big round drops of rain!

Jean ventured forth to see
  How John did fare that day.
She stood aghast and screamed
John's body death-struck lay!

With quiv'ring lips spake Jean,
  "Ma darling, John, but cheep."
He oped his eyes and said
  "Whate'er ye saw, ye reap."

The spirit fled. The dame
  Gazed sadly on the clay
"Wi sair, sair heart, I'll reap
"What's sawn this Sawbath day."

## The Minister Militant

In lonely moorland hope,
  Remote from city strife,
A rev'rend pastor led
  A simple virtuous life.

He tended well his flock,
  He visited the poor,
And conscientiously
  He laboured in his cure.

He vowed he ne'er would cross
  The treach'rous Rubicon;
And Betty was his mate,
  As year by year rolled on.

By Clora's rippling brook
  He lashed his rod and reel;
His hom'lies learned by rote,
  And ofttimes banned the eel.
One harvest afternoon,
  As Stewart's line he plied,
Two stout Hibernians
  Come near him he espied.

Their eyes stared wide to see
  A cleric coat and hat:
And in a trice they leered,
  And gibingly spake Pat.

"Yir rev'rence, where's yer creel?
  "Ye'll spare a little fish;
"We've ta'en the hairst up by-
  "We'll roast them in a dish."

"My friends," the pastor said,
  "I've naither dish nor creel;
"Pass on your ways, good lads;
  "Aye warsel wi' the deil."

"The deil's yirsel', yir togs
 "Were cut o' Clootie's wab,
"And, troth, we'll share yir draw-
 "Mike, on him wi' that stab."

"Ye coward loons," quoth he
 The Rev'rend Thomas Brown
"How daur ye jibe and jeer?"
 His face was all afrown.
In holy rage he doffed
 His coat and eke his hat;
And with firm clenchéd fist
 He thus addresséd Pat

"These marks of holy caste
 "I to the ground affix;
"Nae mair o' gab: come on;
"Tam Broun will gie yer licks."

Then both the harvesters
 Glared fierce into his face,
And backward fell, with oaths:
 Says Mike, "We'll mak' a race."

They ran by Millmount House
 And Rauchie Littledean,
Until the pastor chased
 Them out of parish clean.

Besmired with clotted sweat,
  He sat on Carfrae Bridge;
His eye caught sight of rod
  Afloat on Clora's ridge.

He leapt into the stream;
  His trusty wand he got,
And trudged along the haughs
  To don his hat and coat.
Now, Betty in the manse
  Was sore perturbed that day;
Her rev'rend master out
  And gloaming turned to grey.

She wandered o'er the glebe,
  Drank of the Holy Well,
And hied to Clora Den
  A-racing o'er the fell.

Beside the rippling brook
  She saw the coat and hat;
And breathless all and pale
  She by the twain down sat.

And suddenly she shrieked;
  Dark thoughts her bosom crossed
The Rev'rend Thomas Brown
  His life afishing lost!

She ran from pool to pool;
  Anon she sobbed and screamed,
And now to Millmount House
  To raise alarm she deemed

But ere she reached the Swipe
  The pastor met her view:
With loud lament she cried,
  "Broun Raivrent, is that you?"

"My hairt's been like tae brak'
  "Tae think ye had been droon';
"Am really gled tae see
"Ye lookin' hale and soun'."

The pastor, quite demure,
  Told Betty all the tale
How in his own defence
  He did the loons assail.

Still is story heard
  In Clora's rural Den;
The moral, with a leer,
  That "Ministers are men."

Lauder Train. Reproduced courtesy of Robert D Clapperton, Photographic Trust

# Appendix 2 — Tourist information for the Lauder Light Railway

**Extract from a local guidebook:**

"Though the Lauder Light Railway is comparatively short, the passenger may have in view several scenes of more than local and temporary interest. Channelkirk Church and Manse will call to mind the shepherd lad who watched his flocks on the slopes of the Leader and beheld the glory of Aidan as he joined the angelic choir.

He may catch a glimpse of the road by which Johnny Cope fled to

Coldstream, and Bonnie Prince Charlie led his leal-hearted Highlandmen. He may, between trains, spend a few hours at Oxton to visit Crosschainhill, along the pilgrim's road as far as the Church of the Holy Trinity.

And if he is not ecclesiastic, historian, or antiquarian, let him proceed to the terminus, where he may wander for a week of days on Lauder Common, amid "bonnie braes and wimpling burns," and inhale the invigorating breeze from the wild and stormy Lammermoors.

If he be too old or too lazy to climb, let him in the morning set his watch by the Tolbooth Clock, during the day let him watch the shadows of the "ill-fated favourites" as they sport on the pellucid Leader under the Castle Bridge, and in the evening let him have a few choice burghers in "my favourite shop" to pass the gossip of the town.

And if all these fail to heal his disordered mind, let him make straight endeavour to discover his relationship to that the idle writer who gave the name of "Sleepy Hollow" to one of the more picturesque and pleasing scenes of the Scottish Lowlands.

This done, with ticket and baggage he must needs take an early train, and return to that fool's paradise from whence he came."

# Appendix 3 — Colonel Guinan's Letter

(Information continued from page 90)

Dear Lord Borthwick

August 2000

As an acquaintance of your father through our mutual Army connections, I found our meetings were always a great pleasure. We had a common interest in the Royal Artillery and this was enhanced, of course, by Harry's special regard for the connection with Robert Borthwick, Master Gunner to James IV.

After many years away from Scotland, I came back for a few quiet years in 1995. Sadly, I had only one more, brief, meeting with your father. Soon after that I learned that I had "volunteered" to care for the historical records of several Edinburgh and East of Scotland Gunner units and this moment of weakness has now involved me with a rather wider brief. This, in turn, has led me to develop a catalogue of ephemera into a narrative.

A suitable starting point seemed to be the receipt by James II from a grateful father-in-law of a pair of *bombards, which allows me to mention the gun manufacture at Edinburgh Castle and Robert Borthwick. Your father's notes and letters led me to other sources, which looked sound, until I realised that a casual comment had given me to believe that the lineage from Robert Borthwick to Crookston was established. I had also assumed that Robert Borthwick fell at Flodden in 1513.

Subsequently I found the following in the Proceedings of the

Society of Antiquaries of Scotland Volume 33 (1898-99) Paper V (pp 185-194), "Notice of the King's Master Gunners of Scotland, with the Writs of their Appointments, 1512-1703 – 1512 – Robert Borthuick (sic). He is in Dieppe this year on the King's business, acting under the direction of Andrew, Bishop of Caithness, Receiver of the Kingdom of Scotland. He dies in 1531."

The current draft of the relevant chapter is enclosed and it would be a great help if you can spare a few minutes to look at this, especially the sections I have marked. It is my present intention to deposit the paper in the National War Museum of Scotland (at Edinburgh Castle) with a copy for the R A Institution Historical Trust at Woolwich. If there is a demand for further copies then wider publication may be considered. Please let me know if anything I have written is incorrect, unacceptable or in any , in your view, inappropriate. I do hope that this is not an unwarranted imposition.

Yours sincerely

Tony Guinan

*The first "big guns" are known as "bombards", since their prime use was against masonry and similar fortifications, serving the same purpose as a battering ram.

Extracts from Colonel Guinan's booklet *British Artillery Before 1859*

In 1509, James IV employed Robert Borthwick his master gunner, to cast a set of brass ordnance for The Castle, which had this inscription: "Machina sum, Scoto Borthwick fabricata Roberto." Seven of these cannon were named by the king the Sisters of Borthwick, being remarkable for their beauty and size. When preparing for his fatal invasion of England in 1513, James went daily to The Castle, for the purpose of proving and inspecting his artillery; and it is related that on one of these occasions he narrowly escaped death from the fragments of a culverin that burst by his side.

The Seven Sisters of Borthwick were captured at Flodden, with ten other brass field-pieces, and sent to Berwick; here the Earl of Surrey saw them, and described them as being more beautiful than any other cannon in the arsenal of King Henry.

In May 1573 (while Sir William Kirkaldy was defending Edinburgh Castle on behalf of Mary, Queen of Scots) ships from England having arrived in the Forth with troops and ordnance, siege batteries had been established on all sides, some with guns as large as 100 pounders. A contemporary writer noted that, amongst the cannon landed by Sir William drury, the English commander, was one of the Seven Sisters of Borthwick. After a week of bombardment, the Castle was captured.

# **Bibliography**

Allan, Rev. Archibald, History of Channelkirk (Edinburgh, James Thin, 1900).

Bower, John Junior,  Description of the Abbeys of Melrose and Old Melrose, with their Traditions.  (Kelso, Alexander Leadbetter, 1813).

Cruden, Stewart,  The Scottish Castle.  (Nelson, 1960).

Lauderdale in the 20th Century. (Galashiels, Buccleuch Printers, 2003).

The Scots Magazine. (Dundee).

A.T.G. Lammermoor Leaves. (Galashiels, D Craighead, *Border Advertiser* Office, 1898).

Mackay, John James, Border Highways.  (Kelso, published by John James Mackay and printed by Kelso Graphics, 1998).

Forbes, George, Scottish Battles. (Glasgow, published by Lang Syne Publishers Ltd and printed by Dave Barr Print, 2001).

Clancy, Thomas Owen (Editor), The Triumph Tree. (Edinburgh, published by Canongate Books, 1998).

Ogilvie, Will H, The Border Poems.  (Hawick, Reproduced by the Hawick News, 1998).

# BIBLIOGRAPHY

Moffat, Brian, A Series of Reports on Researches into the Medieval Hospital at Soutra. (5 Fala Village, Lothian, EH37 5SY, published by SHARP).

Armit, Ian, Celtic Scotland. (London, published by B T Batsford / Historic Scotland, 2005).

Wilson, John, Mackay, Wilson's Tales of the Borders. (Edinburgh & London, published by The Murray Press, 1934)

Elliot, Walter, The New Minstrelsy of the Scottish Border 1805 – 2005. (Selkirk, Published by Deerpark Press Ltd, 2006).

# List of Illustrations

Plate 1: Oxton painted by John Mackay. Reproduced courtesy of Liz Maddock.

Plate 2: Drawing of Oxton Village by John Mackay, 1974.

Plate 3: Looking down Upper Lauderdale with Scots Pine trees in foreground.

Plate 4: Part of the Fort on Dere Street lying NNW from Kirktonhill. In the foreground is a farm vehicle track.

Plate 5: Aerial Photo of Oxton Fort. Annfield Inn in background. Taken August 1956. University of Cambridge Photo Library Collection.

Plate 6: Part of the earthworks of the Celtic hillfort at Kirktonhill.

Plate 7: St Cuthbert and the Otters. Photograph of Woodcarving by Elizabeth Strachan Dempster, circa 1950. Royal Scottish Academy Collection.

Plate 8: The ruins of Restlaw Ha'.

Plate 9: Excavating Soutra Hospital. Reproduced courtesy of Brian Moffat.

Plate 10: Soutra Aisle before restoration. Reproduced courtesy of Brian Moffat.

Plate 11: Photograph of cup and ring stone found near Soutra Hospital.

Plate 12: Carfraemill, circa 1910. Reproduced courtesy of Robert D Clapperton, Photograghic Trust

Plate 13: New Channelkirk from A68 road. The Kings Road runs along the valley floor on the far side of the farm buildings.

Plate 14: The 13th century watermill at Mountmill.

Plate 15: Channelkirk Church.

Plate 16: Channelkirk Manse.

Plate 17: Kirk House.

Plate 18: Letter written in 1768 by David Scott, minister at Channelkirk to Alexander Low, merchant at Fala. Reproduced courtesy of Lindsay Errington.

Plate 19: Snow Picture of Oxton Village, February 2001.

Plate 20: Snow Picture with Channelkirk Cottage in foreground and Church in background, February 2001.

Plate 21: View of Channelkirk Church and graveyard looking at southwest corner of church. Reproduced courtesy of the *Southern Reporter.*

Plate 22: Grave of shepherd and his dog in Channelkirk graveyard at SW corner of church.

Plate 23: Grave of Marian Brock.

Plate 24: Grave of Archibald Allan at door of Church. The grave is enclosed by a low railing and is the grave on the left.

Plate 25: The plaque to the Sower in the wall of the steading at Threeburnford.

Plate 26: Looking down Upper Lauderdale, January 1979. Blue-grey cows on the left with New Channelkirk behind. Channelkirk Cottages in the centre distance. Glengelt lies to the right of the trees in the foreground. Reproduced courtesy of John Wilkie.

Plate 27: Glengelt House. The Soutra Plateau runs along the skyline.

Plate 28: The Master Gunner, Robert Borthwick, fell to his knees and implored the King to let him open fire on the English Army at Flodden. Picture painted by John Mackay.

Plate 29: Snowplough tries to clear blocked road on Soutra in 1957. Reproduced courtesy of Scotsman Publications Ltd.

Plate 30: Braefoot at the junction of Kirktonhill and Hartside roads.

Plate 31: Old Inchkeith Steading.

Plate 32: Railway Station, Oxton after 1910. The driver is standing on the train's footplate. © The Trustees of the National Museums of Scotland.

Plate 33: Main Street, Oxton 1931. Reproduced courtesy of RCAHMS (R S Henderson)

Plate 34: The Main Street, Oxton, in the 1880s, showing the Tower Hotel as a thatched cottage.

Plate 35: View of the upper part of The Row, Oxton.

Plate 36: Jock and Dod Campbell outside Oxton Castle with unknown lady, early 1920s. Reproduced courtesy of Flora Pretswell.

Plate 37: John Brown from Oxton Mains with pair of horse outside Smiddy in Main Street, Oxton, early 1940s. The burnt-out shell of Oxton Castle can be seen in the background. Reproduced courtesy of Flora Pretswell.

Plate 38: Oxton War Memorial Hall on the left with Justicehall in the baekground.

Plate 39: Jim and Elsie Gilchrist at their Diamond Wedding in March 1989.

Plate 40: Cockburn's Shop in Station Road, Oxton. Photograph possibly taken in early 1930s. Photographer unknown.

Plate 41: Beverley Dorward and Jim Harris outside the Bakehouse Store, Oxton. Reproduced courtesy of William Brodie.

Plate 42: George Bell with his grocer's van on his last round before retirement.

Plate 43: View looking up from the bottom of The Row. The old village hall is the two-storey building on the left.

Plate 44: View from The Loan, Oxton, circa 1938. Business names in view include The Tower Hotel; J M Matthewson, stationer & newsagent. Reproduced courtesy of the University of St Andrews Library.

Plate 45: Tossing the Caber at Oxton games, August 1936. R Harkness tossing the cable, and the judge making notes. Scottish Borders Council, Museum and Gallery Service Collection.

Map 1: The Parish of Channelkirk in Lauderdale by John Mackay, 1974.

Map 2: Channelkirk Church and surrounding area. © Crown Copyright and/or database right. All rights reserved. Licence No. 100046429

Map 3: Oxton and surrounding area. © Crown Copyright and/or database right. All rights reserved. Licence No. 100046429

# Index

Terms in brackets after some Borthwicks in the index refer to my relationship to them.

Agricola, Julius(p13,16); Aidan, Bishop(p21,22,51); Airhouse(p28,29,61,67,119); Airhouse Quarry(p97,98); Aldun, Bishop(p24); Alexander II(p39,41); Allan, Rev.Archibald(p41,44,55,56,57,59,60,69,75,80); Ancrum(p33); Anderson, Bob(p102,103); Annfield Inn(p16,122,123); Armet, River(p82); Armstrong's map(p29).

Bairns Cundie(p64,65); Bannockburn, Battle of(p43); Bartlett, John(p71); Beattie, Mary(p67); Bell, Dod(p69,70); Bell, George(p99,105,121,126); Bell, Tom(p126); Bennet, Josh(p105); Bernham, Bishop de(p41,42); Bernicia(p19); Berwick(p29,40,103,118); Black Bull Hotel, Lauder(p108); Blackburn(p98); Black Hill(p82); Blackshiels(p55,108); Blaeu's Atlas(p40); Blair Tony(p58); Boisil(see St Boisil); Border Telegraph(p128); Borthwick Castle(p52); Borthwick, Elspeth(p25,38,61,73,77,91,97,102,119,121,123,125); Borthwick, Lord Harry(father)(p34,89,90); Borthwick, Henry(grandfather)(p80); Borthwick, John(great great-uncle)(p95,103); Borthwick, Lord John(brother)(p89,96); Borthwick, Lord John(p52); Borthwick, Sir John(p52); Borthwick, Malcolm(p38,61,125); Borthwick, Michael(p79); Borthwick, Rev.Ninian(p51); Borthwick, Robert(p88,89,90); Borthwick, Third Lord of(p89); Borthwick, William(great grandfather)(p34); Borthwick, Lord William(p79); Borthwick, Sir William(p79); Bowerhouse(p99,100,101); Bower, John(p23); Brady, Ian(p125); Brae Cottage(p102); Braefoot(p69,95); Brock, Marian(p68); Brock, William(p68); Brown, Cecil(p127); Brown, Rev.John(p44,45); Brown, Mrs(p17); Burnfoot(p69); Burrell, John(p69); Burrell, William(p117,118); Butterdean(p17).

Campbell, Dod(p113); Campbell, Jock(p113); Campbells of Oxton(p113,114); Capes, Goeff(p125); Carfrae(p43,71,82,119); Carfraemill(p36,37,58,83,92,122): Carter Bar(p35); Carver, Keith(p126); Catterick(p20); Channelkirk(p9,11,13,16,19,21,27,28,35,39,40,41,43,45,46,48,49,51,5

2,53,54,55,56,57,58,59,60,61,63,64,66,67,70,76,79,86,87,88,
89,113,128); Channelkirk Church(p16,17,28,39,40,41,42,43,44,
45,46,48,49,52,55,56,58,61,69,71,73,128); Channelkirk
Cottage(p58,73,74); Channelkirk Cottages(p77);
Channelkirk Farm(p48); Channelkirk House/Manse
(p46,47,48,49,58,75); Channelkirk Inn(p38,75);
Channelkirk School(p99,110,113,128,129); Channelkirk
Village(p17,73,87); Charles I(p40,52,56,67,85); Charles II(p85);
Clints Hill(p29); Clorabank(p110,113); Clora Burn(p113); Coaevus
Monachies(p26); Cockburn, Rev.Henry(p52);
Cockburnspath(p34);Cockburn's trading business(p117,118);
Coldstream(p38,87); Collielaw(p98); Collie Law(p11); Colman,
Bishop(p22); Connery, Sir Sean(p102); Cope, Sir John(p75);
Crombie Smith, Dr Harry(p77,110); Crombie Smith, Dr John(p110);
Cromwell, Oliver(p52,85); Crookston(p98,103,106); Cuthbert (see
St Cuthbert); Cuthell, Tom(p40).

Dalkeith(p80,92,99,100,103,107,108); David II(p32,34); Dean
Bridge(p86); Demster, Elizabeth Strachan(p26); Den, The(see
Lourie's Den); Denholm, Alec(p122); Dere Street(p13,16,
29,35,36,38,62,82,93); Dewer,John(p67); Dorward, Beverley(p121);
Douglas, Bill(p126); Douglas, David(p126); Dryburgh
Abbey(p32,39,43); Dunbar(p75,85,86); Dundas, Sir James of
Arniston(p79); Dun Law(p92,93); Duns(p87,101,115);
Durham(p23,25,26,27,89).

Earlston(p47,82,101,107); Eata(p22); Edinburgh(p9,13,20,25,29,
31,40,46,53,56,75,76,79,85,86,87,92,99,102,103,115,117,121); Edward
II(p43); Eildon Hills(p16,82); Elliot, Walter(p20,21,33); Errington,
Dr Lindsay(p55); Eskbank(p106).

Faa-Blyth, Charles(p82); Faa, Johnny(p81); Faa tribe(p81);
Fairnylees(p83,119); Fala(p9,16,54,55); Fallen, John(p92); Farne
Islands(p23); Flodden, battle of(p86,87,88,89,90); Flynns,
The(p98); Fordyce, Rev.Francis(p48); Forth(p13,19,20);
Fountainhall(p80,103,105,106,107); Friar's Nose(p67,119);
Fullerton, Bill(p119); Fullerton, Jim(p121).

Galashiels(p47,60,126); Gala Water(p32,106); Gilchrist,
Andy(p118); Gilchrist, Billy(p115); Gilchrist, Dod(p115); Gilchrist,
Doreen(p115); Gilchrist, James(p106,117); Gilchrist,

John(p28,65,69,70,102,103); Gilston(p34); Girth Gate(p29,82,101); Glasgow(p53,118); Glengelt(p11,21,38,43,52,65,67,79,80,119,122); Graham, Gibbie(p123); Graham Laura(p123); Graham, William(p123); Greenlaw(p38,58); Groves, Lilian(p27); Guinan, Colonel A(p89,90).

Haddington(p65,66,99); Hamilton, Duke of(p52); Hardie, Robert(p83); Harkins, Danny(p98); Harris, Jim(p121); Hartside(p29,77,95,98,101,105); Hawick(p33,128); Headshaw(p11,36,37,38,52,67,82,83,119); Headshaw Hill(p11); Heart of Midlothian FC(p114,115); Heathfield(p123); Henderson, David(p54); Henry VIII(p86,87); Heriotshiels(p76); Herring Way(p86); Hibernian FC(p118); Hillhouse(p19,119); Historic Scotland(p13); Hogarth, Jimmy(p98); Hog Hill(p11); Hogg, Potato Merchant(p99); Holy Water Cleugh(p28); Hospital of the Holy Trinity(p31); Humber(p20); Humbie(p9,55); Hume, Andy(p100); Hume, Will(p70); Hunter, Agnes(p80); Hunters Hall(p13,36,80, also see Lourie's Den); Hutton Castle(p117).

Inchkeith(p101); Iona(p22).

James II(p79); James IV(p81,86,87,88); James, Rev.Richard(p48,61); Jedburgh(p39); Jefferies, Jim(p114); Jicha, Vaclav(p65,66); Justicehall(p106,115,117); Justice, Captain James(p115,117); Justice, Judge James(p115); Justice Park(p128).

Kate's Cauldron(p90,91); Kellet, Drew(p47); Kelphope(p83); Kelso(p49,75); King's Inch(p82); King's Road(p37); Kirkcudbright(p26); Kirk House(p47,48); Kirk O'Shotts Primary School(p27); Kirktonhill(p16,19,52,58,62,69,74,76,77,95,119,123); Kirk Yetholm(p82); Knox, Jack(p126).

Laing, Jimmy(p101); Lammer Law(p83,85); Lammermuir(p9,11,34,70,84); Landells, Ian(p74); Lauder(p9,11,40,47,48,49,51,61,65,74,75,77,84,90,98,103,105,106,107,108,115,119,125,128); Lauderdale(p9,13,21,32,39,40,43,57,60,80,82,85,86,101,102); Lauderdale, John(p60); Lauderdale, Second Earl of(p40,83,84,85); Lauder Light Railway(p74,103,104,105,106,107,108); Lauder Station(p106); Leader(p11,22,36,47,82,83,87,109); Lees, David(p65); Leith(p86); Liddell, Rev.David(p52,53); Liddell, Henry

Marchall(p69,113); Liddell, Provost of Dalkeith(p108); Lindesfarne(p21,22,23,26,28); Lindores(p47); Linn Dean(p90,91); Liuska, Juliette(p65,66); London(p38,56,84,85,103); Longden, Ann(p73,74); Lourie's Den(p65,80,81,101, also see Hunters Hall); Low, Alexander(p54,55); Lylestone, Margaret(p83).

McConnachie, Mrs(p48); McDonald, Alec(p115,118); McGahey, Mick(p125); Mackay, John(p61,82,83,102,104); Mackay, John James(p35); Mackay, Kay(p102); Mackay, Mrs(p47); McLeod, Ally(p114); McNeil, George(p125); Maddock, Liz(p121); Malcolm IV(p31); Marischal College(p53); Matthewson, Roualeyn William(p123,128); Meadowbank(p126); Melrose(p17,18,22,23,26,28,29,32); Melrose Abbey(p23,27,28); Midburn Farm(p99); Middletoun(p98); Midside Maggie(p83,84,85); Miller, Ernie(p49,97,106,123); Mitchell, Bertie(p98); Moffat, Dr Brian(p32,33,40); Morpeth(p38); Mortimer, Katherine(p32); Mountmill(p43,46,69); Mundeville, Sir Henry de(p43); Murray, Colonel David(p76); Murray, Mrs Rosemary(p76); Murray, Rev.Thomas(p56); Musselburgh(p125).

National Museum of Antiquities(p85);Nether Howden(p102); Nevill's Cross, battle of(p34); Newbattle Abbey(p29,79); Newbyres(p79); Newcastle(p38,92); New Channelkirk(p11,37,38,75,77,91,119); Newstead(p16); Nisbet, Billy(p126); Nisbet, Willie(p114); Northumbria(p20,22).

Ogilvie, Will H(p18); Old Fish Road(p86); Osborn, Kevin(p91); Osborn, Mary(p91); Otterburn, battle of(p35); Overhowden(p19); Oxton(p9,11,28,45,47,49,58,65,69,70,71,76,82,83,95,97,98,99,101,102,103,104,105,106,107,108,109,113,115,117,119,121,122,123,125,126,127,128); Oxton Bovial Society(p127,128); Oxton Castle(p113); Oxton Professional Games(p125); Oxton Quoiting Challenge Cup(p126,127); Oxton Reel(p125); Oxton Station(p104,105,106); Oxton Total Abstinence Society(p127); Oxton War Memorial Hall(p45,48,61,92,122,125).

Pathhead(p11,13,16,86,107,108); Pathhead Bridge(p86);Peebles(p97); Preston, The baker(p121); Prestonpans, battle of(p75); Pringle Mary(p79); Purves, Andrew(p99,100); Purves Billy(p99); Purves, Davy(p113);

Reid, James and Alexander(p95,128); Restlaw Ha'(p29); Rigside(p127); Ripon(p22,24); Roman Heritage Centre, Melrose(p18); Romano Bridge(p81); Rothbury(p81); Rous, Francis(p53); Rowe, Tom(p99); Roxburghshire(p13,32); Royal Observer Corps(p90); Royal Scottish Academy(p25); Rutherford, Rev.James(p55,56); Rutherfurd's Southern Counties' Register and Directory(p127).

St Aidan (see Aidan, Bishop); St Andrews, Bishop of(p41); St Boisil(p22,82); St Boswells(p22,82); St Conal(p40); St Cuthbert(p21,22,23,24,25,26,27,28,39,51,89,92); St Cuthberts View(p128); St Leonards(p16); St Mary's School(p28); Sandilands, Alec(p119,121); Sandilands, Eddie(p121); Sandilands, Mount(p121); Scone(p85); Scotsman newspaper(p27,48,59,76,80,106,107); Scots Magazine(p61,82,83,102,104); Scott, Rev.David(p54,55); Scott, Dod(p69); Scott, Mary(p117,123); Scott, Mrs(p74); Scott, Sir Walter(p22,25,87,88); Scott, Willie(p74); Scottish National Heritage(p90); Selkirk(p126); Shaw tribe(p81); Shields, Rev.John(p49); Shields, Mary(p49); Shielfield(p105); Sibbald, Sir Robert(p40); Small, Dr Leonard(p41); Sommerville, George(p67); Southern Reporter(p31,47,92,99,102,126); Soutra(p13,29,31,32,33,34,35,38,52,57,80,82,85,86,90,91,92,97,98, 101,108,128); Soutra Aisle(p31,32,34,82); Soutra Edge(p35,62); Soutra Hill(p13,36,57,90,92,108); Soutra Hospital/Hospice(p31,32,33); Soutra Plateau(p9,11,13,37,82,85,92); Spence, James(p117); Spence Mrs(p117); Steele, Billy(p58); Stewart, Captain(p47); Stewart, Elspeth(p67); Stewart, Mrs(p47,76); Stobs(p79); Stow(p9,56,57,67,90,106); Stuart, Charles Edward(p75,81); Sunday Post(p115); Surrey, Lord(p89); Sutherland, Ian(p38,119); Sutherland, Dr Mary(p77).

Tattie picking(p99,100,101); Tees(p13,19); Telford, Thomas(p85,86); Thirlestane(p52,75,84,85); Threeburnford(p20,32,70,103); Tiberius, Emperor(p17); Tollishill(p19,83,85,119); Tower Hotel(p99,102,110,114); Trabroun(p20); Trimontium(p16,17); Turf Law(p11,13,65); Turnpike Act(p36); Tweed, river(p87); Tyne, river(p25); Tyne Water(p86).

Ugston(p64,68,109); Upper Lauderdale(p11,13,83).

Venerable Bede(p21,23); Victoria, Queen(p80).

Waldie, Dave(p32,126); Walker, Adam(p67); Walker,
Rev.James(p46,47); Warner, Beth(p128); Warner Charles(p128);
Warner Dudley(p128); Waterston, James(p67); Weir, David(p97);
Weir Isa(p96,97); Weir Johnny(p96,97); Westruther(p84);
Whitby(p22); Wilkinson, Derek(p101); Wilkinson, Janet(p101);
Wilkinson, John(p101); Windy Cleugh(p65); Wooler(p38);
Woolwich(p89); Worcester, battle of(p40,84,85).

York(p16,109); Young, Bob(p82); Young, Robert(p114).